# The Career Woman's Guide to Improving Success, Confidence, Assertiveness and Achievements.

A Modern Woman's Guide to Confidence, Self-Esteem, Assertiveness, Empowerment, Achievement and Success.

**Arianna Blakely**

By reading this document, the reader agrees that under no circumstances is the author responsible for any losses, direct or indirect, that are incurred as a result of the use of the information contained within this document, including, but not limited to, errors, omissions, or inaccuracies.

# Table of Contents

# Part 1 — Unlocking Success: Navigating Obstacles & The Fine Print On Your Journey To Executive Presence

# Introduction

## Embracing Confidence & Assertiveness As A Woman

Imagine a young woman who, for years, struggled with self-doubt and the fear of speaking up. She always blended into the background, afraid of drawing attention to herself. While her male colleagues confidently advanced in their careers, she remained stagnant, yearning for the courage to step into her own power. Thankfully, a turning point came when she attended a seminar on confidence and assertiveness. Inspired by the stories of women who had overcome similar struggles, she embarked on a personal transformational journey. She gained the confidence to express her thoughts through self-reflection, challenging limiting beliefs and developing effective communication skills. She set boundaries that honored her needs and values.

Now, as that woman and the author of this book, I want to share my story and the valuable lessons I learned, guiding you toward embracing your innate confidence and assertiveness.

Confidence and assertiveness are essential qualities that empower women to navigate their lives with strength, resilience, and self-assurance. However, many women in today's society grapple with a lack of confidence and struggle to assert themselves effectively. This book is here to guide you on a transformative journey toward cultivating the confidence and assertiveness you deserve.

Women often ask why they lag behind their male counterparts regarding confidence and assertiveness. The reasons are complex, rooted in societal expectations and contrasting cultural norms that shape the upbringing of girls compared to boys. Throughout history, girls have been encouraged to embody traits such as politeness, compliance, and self-sacrifice, while boys are urged to be assertive, bold, and competitive. These differences in upbringing can lead to ingrained beliefs that hinder the development of self-assurance and assertiveness in women, perpetuating a confidence gap between genders.

Research reveals that these disparities affect women's confidence and assertiveness in adulthood. Women are less likely to negotiate for higher salaries and promotions, tend to underestimate their abilities, and are more prone to imposter syndrome. These patterns do not indicate any inherent deficiency in women but reflect systemic barriers and societal expectations that limit their growth.

The impact of a lack of confidence and assertiveness on women's lives is significant. It may hold you back from pursuing your dreams and settling for less than you deserve in your career, relationships, and personal life. Stress, self-doubt, and dissatisfaction may prevail, hindering your overall well-being and success.

However, I want to congratulate you on recognizing the need for change. This book aims to break through the barriers that hold women back, providing you with the tools, strategies, and insights to cultivate unwavering confidence and assertiveness. We will explore the factors contributing to a lack of confidence in women, including cultural expectations, internalized beliefs, and limited access to resources and opportunities.

I will guide your transformation by drawing from the experiences and stories of successful women who have overcome their confidence challenges. We will delve into topics such as self-reflection, challenging limiting beliefs, developing effective communication skills, and establishing healthy boundaries. Through practical exercises and actionable strategies, we will explore the power of positive self-talk, embrace failure as a steppingstone to growth, and harness the strength of vulnerability to authentically connect with others.

Embracing confidence and assertiveness as a woman yields profound benefits, including increased self-worth, unlocked opportunities, fulfillment, and the ability to inspire others. Confident women advance careers, negotiate better salaries, and enjoy healthier relationships. It's important to remember that confidence and assertiveness are not qualities reserved for a select few. They are skills that can be learned, honed, and integrated into daily life. By embracing the principles and practices outlined in this book, you will remake yourself and contribute to a broader cultural shift that values and supports confident and assertive women.

It's time to take ownership of your life and embrace your innate power. Know that it's okay to celebrate your achievements, prioritize self-care, and contribute to a cultural shift that values confident women. By embracing the principles in this book, you can transform yourself and continue the journey toward empowerment and equality. Together, let's honor the struggles of women throughout history and their fight for equality.

So, are you ready to embark on this empowering journey toward becoming the confident, assertive woman you are meant to be? Are you prepared to achieve your full potential, unleash your authentic voice, and create the life you deserve?

If your answer is a resounding **HELL YES!**, then let us begin. Get ready to unlock your inner strength, challenge the status quo, and support one another on this remarkable path to confidence and assertiveness. Throughout the pages of this book, we will navigate the challenges, celebrate the victories, and empower each other to embrace our true potential. Together, we will rise as confident, assertive women and as catalysts for change in our communities and the world.

Now is the time to take that first step. Turn the page, and let the transformation begin. Your journey to embracing confidence and assertiveness starts now.

# Chapter 1: Confidence &

# Assertiveness Challenges

# For Women In The Modern

# Era

"Fine print" encompasses hidden details that can significantly influence our progress, alter agreements, or limit our negotiation ability. By demonstrating assertiveness and confidence, you can empower yourself to clarify the specifics, ensuring that you position yourself best for what you want from life. Whether in your job or another area of your life, developing increased assertiveness and confidence skills can empower you to advocate for terms and conditions that align with your goals, ultimately securing something that fulfills your needs.

The following points outline some areas you must learn about and be aware of, as they can affect your confidence and assertiveness levels.

# Having An Executive Presence

Female executive presence refers to qualities, behaviors, and characteristics that convey confidence, authority, and influence in professional settings. It encompasses how women carry themselves, communicate, and engage with others, particularly in leadership or executive roles. Confidence and assertiveness play essential roles in developing an executive presence for women.

### Confidence

Confidence is a fundamental aspect of executive presence. It involves having faith in one's abilities, skills, and knowledge. Confident women project a strong sense of self-assurance, evident in their body language, speech, and overall demeanor. They believe in their capacity to lead, make decisions, and handle challenging situations effectively.

### Assertiveness

Assertiveness is about expressing one's thoughts, opinions, and needs clearly and directly while respecting the perspectives of others. Assertive women communicate confidently, advocate for themselves, and assert their authority when necessary. They are unafraid to contribute to discussions, take risks, or challenge the status quo.

It's important to note that executive presence for women is not about mimicking male behavior or adopting a singular leadership style. It involves embracing one's unique strengths, developing a leadership style that aligns with personal values, and effectively navigating professional environments while maintaining authenticity and integrity. Confidence and assertiveness are integral components that contribute to women's overall presence and influence in executive positions.

# Unveiling Unseen Challenges On The Path To Executive Presence

## • The Confidence Gap

The confidence gap for women stems from a complex interplay of factors, including societal expectations, limited representation, gender bias, and the fear of judgment. Historically, women have been socialized to be more modest and accommodating, which can lead to a diminished sense of self-assurance. The lack of female role models in leadership positions further reinforces this gap, making it difficult for women to envision themselves as confident leaders. Gender biases, often subtle and implicit, cast doubt on women's abilities and behaviors, causing them to question their competence. Additionally, the fear of being labeled as "bossy" or "aggressive" discourages assertiveness. By understanding and addressing these underlying challenges, you can work towards closing the confidence gap and fostering a stronger sense of self-assured leadership.

### *Societal Expectations – Louisa May Alcott*

Louisa May Alcott, the remarkable author of "Little Women," defied societal norms and confronted the limitations imposed on women in the late 1800s. With her intelligence, outspokenness, and remarkable confidence, Alcott resented the gender-based rules that constrained girls. Despite societal expectations, she boldly pursued her passion for writing and earned a living crafting bloodstained gothic thrillers under the pseudonym A.M. Barnard. However, the prevailing attitudes of the time towards women's writing forced Alcott to shift her focus to more socially acceptable works like, "Little Women."

Through her remarkable journey, Alcott exemplified women's struggle in a society that restricted their creative expression and limited their opportunities. Her evolution from writing gothic thrillers to crafting the enduring classic, "Little Women" is a testament to her talent and the pressures women experienced to conform to societal expectations. Alcott's story is a powerful reminder of the obstacle's women have overcome and continue to face in their pursuit of self-expression and equality.

Throughout history, societal norms and expectations have limited women's opportunities and defined their roles. Women have often been socialized to be more modest, accommodating, and less assertive, which can undermine their confidence. These gendered expectations shape women's self-perception and behavior, creating a belief that they must work harder to prove themselves and be less confident in their abilities.

Today, we confront obstacles such as pay inequality, limited access to modern technology, and fewer resources for entrepreneurship. One of the main challenges women encounter today is the persistence of gender inequality, that persistent "glass ceiling" still hampers progress.

## *Lack Of Representation*

Limited representation of women in leadership positions and other traditionally male-dominated fields can contribute to the confidence gap. When women don't see others like them in positions of authority or success, it can be challenging to envision themselves in similar roles. The absence of role models and mentors affects their confidence in pursuing ambitious career paths.

Although there has been progress regarding increased representation in leadership positions, gender-based occupational segregation remains prevalent. Men continue to dominate positions of power in various fields. For instance, in 2015, men held 98% of all construction jobs, despite comprising only 53% of the workforce. They were architects, CEOs of building firms, and builders, while less than 10% of women were hired as architectural engineers.

According to the Equitable Growth website, occupational segregation based on gender occurs not due to an efficient allocation of innate talent but rather due to assumptions about the kinds of work different genders are best suited for. This segregation stems from gender stereotypes and preconceived notions about suitable roles, often resulting in women not being matched with or applying for jobs with unique qualifications.

## Gender Bias & Stereotyping

Perpetuating the idea that men are more competent and authoritative while women are more nurturing and supportive is persistent gender stereotyping and biases. These biases can undermine women's confidence by making them question their abilities. Often women will encounter implicit bias in performance evaluations and double standards in their behavior and leadership style. Moreover, stereotypes of assertive women often portray them as "bossy," "aggressive," or "bitchy."

Women are very aware of these stereotypes. Unfortunately, we often try to avoid being negatively labeled through self-censorship and a reluctance to speak up. This leads to a negative cycle where we lack opportunities for meaningful participation, exclusion from decision-making processes, or being overlooked in meetings, further eroding confidence.

## Imposter Syndrome

Imposter syndrome disproportionately affects women and is characterized by persistent self-doubt and fear of being exposed as a fraud despite evidence of competence. Women may attribute their successes to luck or external factors rather than acknowledging their capabilities. This can then lead to diminished confidence in their abilities.

## Perfectionism & Fear Of Judgment

Failure to try, concerning women's confidence and assertiveness, refers to the reluctance or hesitation women may experience in taking risks, pursuing opportunities, or asserting themselves due to fear of failure or negative outcomes. It is a phenomenon influenced by various factors, including societal expectations, gender norms, and the potential consequences of deviating from them. The fear of failure can undermine women's confidence and hinder their ability to be assertive in professional settings.

Addressing these confidence and assertiveness challenges is essential for empowering women in the modern era. By recognizing the societal barriers and biases, women can actively work towards overcoming them, developing their executive presence, and advocating for their goals and aspirations. Through increased confidence and assertiveness, women can assert their rightful place in leadership positions, break glass ceilings, and pave the way for a more inclusive and equitable future.

## • Other Notable Barriers

### *Societal Pressure, Marriage, & Motherhood As A Measure Of Female Success*

Women also face societal expectations and biases that can undermine their assertiveness in the workplace, particularly if they decide to have children. The choice to become a working mother often brings about challenges such as limited maternity leave policies, insufficient support for childcare, and the perception that women should prioritize family over career advancement.

Additionally, childcare and household responsibilities disproportionately fall on women, leading to an increased mental and emotional load that can impact their confidence and assertiveness at work and in their personal lives. This added pressure can make it more difficult for women to advocate for themselves, negotiate promotions or salary increases, and assert their professional boundaries.

Although the barriers to assertiveness for women may have diminished compared to Alcott's era, when women were expected to be demure and solely focused on attracting a suitable husband, remnants of these beliefs persist today. Reality television shows and streaming programs like "Married at First Sight," "Love is Blind," and "The Ultimatum-Marriage" continue to prioritize marriage as the ultimate goal for women. The immense popularity of these shows raises questions about the extent of the progress we have indeed made.

Many women aged 25 and older face pressure from various sources—parents, friends, clergy, and co-workers—to conform to traditional gender roles and become wives and mothers. They are often told they won't feel complete until they have a spouse and children. Society perpetuates the false narrative that marriage and children are necessary for a woman's happiness and success. This pressure can lead to feelings of panic, frustration, and heartbreak for those who don't fit within these expectations.

### *The Result?*

Recognizing and understanding women's challenges in the modern era is crucial for promoting gender equality. Research has shown that, due to these barriers, women are less likely to assert themselves in large groups or meetings. They may quickly apologize for things that are not their responsibility and tend to downplay their own achievements.

While progress has been made, studies on executive presence and confidence in the workplace reveal persistent challenges for women. Despite evidence showing that companies with a significant number of female employees outperform their competitors in terms of profitability, men still maintain a noticeable advantage in confidence within the workforce. This confidence gap translates into higher salaries, more frequent promotions, and better negotiation outcomes for men, creating barriers for women to effectively assert themselves.

# Assertiveness Is Not Bitchiness

*"I want every little girl who's been told she's bossy to be told again she has leadership skills."*

*- Sheryl Sandberg, author and Facebook COO*

Female assertiveness refers to the ability of women to express their thoughts, opinions, needs, and boundaries while maintaining respect confidently and directly for others. It is a quality that empowers women to stand up for themselves, assert their rights, and take action to achieve their goals.

Assertiveness is a positive and necessary trait that contributes to effective communication, healthy relationships, and personal growth. It is essential to dispel the misconception that assertiveness equates to aggression or being a "bitch." Assertiveness is not aggression. While assertiveness involves being direct and firm, it does not include disrespecting or demeaning others. It is a balanced approach that respects boundaries, values diverse perspectives, and aims for mutually beneficial outcomes. Assertive women strive for open and honest communication while fostering positive relationships and collaborative environments.

# Characteristics Of Positive Female Assertiveness

- **Clear Communication**

Assertive women communicate their thoughts, feelings, and expectations clearly and directly without resorting to passive or aggressive communication styles (we will cover communication styles in more detail in the chapter 3). They express themselves respectfully and confidently, ensuring their message is understood while valuing the opinions and perspectives of others.

Example: *In a team meeting, a woman confidently shares her ideas and suggestions for improving a project, using assertive language and tone to express her viewpoint while actively listening to others' feedback.*

- **Boundary Setting**

Assertive women effectively establish and communicate their personal and professional boundaries. They clearly understand what is acceptable to them and express their limits in a firm but respectful manner. They advocate for themselves and protect their interests without disregarding the needs of others.

*Example: A woman firmly communicates to her colleagues that she cannot take on additional tasks outside her scope of work, clearly explaining her workload and priorities without feeling guilty or apologetic.*

- **Self-Advocacy**

Assertive women advocate for their own needs, rights, and interests. They are comfortable asserting their value and contributions to ensure they are not overlooked or taken for granted. They are confident in asking for what they deserve, whether it is a promotion, a fair salary, or recognition for their achievements.

*Example: During a performance review, a woman confidently presents her accomplishments, providing evidence of her contributions and requesting fair recognition and consideration for advancement opportunities.*

- **Active Listening & Assertive Response**

Assertive women actively listen to others, seeking to understand their perspectives, and respond assertively without becoming passive or aggressive. They engage in constructive dialogue, express disagreements respectfully, and find collaborative solutions.

*Example: In a team discussion, a woman actively listens to a colleague's differing opinion, acknowledges their viewpoint, and assertively presents her own perspective, supporting it with logical reasoning and evidence while maintaining a respectful tone.*

- **Confidence In Decision-Making**

Assertive women trust their abilities to make decisions and take ownership of the outcomes. They make choices based on their expertise, intuition, and values without seeking constant validation or approval from others.

*Example: A woman confidently makes a crucial business decision, considering relevant factors, consulting with stakeholders, and taking responsibility for the outcome without second-guessing herself or relying solely on others' opinions.*

Dispelling misconceptions about assertiveness requires promoting understanding and recognizing that assertive women are not "bitches" or overly aggressive. They are confident individuals who navigate professional and personal interactions with respect, self-assurance, and a focus on achieving positive outcomes for themselves and others.

## Up Next?

Explore the transformative power of confidence and assertiveness. Discover how cultivating these traits not only empowers women to overcome barriers but also unlocks a world of opportunities, fosters personal growth, and paves the way for success in both professional and personal spheres. Get ready to unleash your true potential and embrace the countless benefits that confidence and assertiveness can bring.

# Chapter 2: Get Ready To

# Catch The Transformation

# Bug

Creating an assertive and confident attitude is a game-changer for us women. It's our ticket to breaking free from societal expectations and unleashing our true potential. When you embrace assertiveness, something magical happens – your self-confidence soars. You courageously speak up, set boundaries, and demand the respect you deserve. No longer confined by traditional gender roles, you can chase your dreams with unwavering determination. Living assertively ensures that your needs are met, personally and professionally, without compromise. Say goodbye to conflicts and stress as you confidently express your thoughts and emotions, fostering healthier relationships. Best of all, assertiveness nourishes your overall well-being, empowering you to prioritize self-care, establish boundaries, and pursue happiness. So, ladies, it's time to embrace the power of assertiveness, unlock your full potential, and inspire others to do the same. The world is waiting for you to shine.

*"We must have perseverance and above all confidence in ourselves. We must believe that we are gifted for something and that this thing must be attained."*
*— Marie Curie, pioneer of science and Nobel Laureate.*

# How Assertiveness Empowers Women To Thrive

As women, we have often been encouraged to adopt passive behaviors, conforming to societal expectations by being accommodating and avoiding conflict. Passive behavior is characterized by a reluctance to express our thoughts, needs, and boundaries openly. It involves staying silent, suppressing our genuine emotions, and prioritizing the desires and opinions of others over our own. Society has ingrained in us that being agreeable and submissive is the only path to acceptance and approval. However, it is time for us to challenge these notions and embrace the power of assertiveness.

Assertiveness is a transformative quality that enables us to confidently express ourselves while respecting the rights of others. It is the antithesis of passivity, empowering us to break free from the limitations imposed by societal expectations. By embodying assertiveness, we can experience a multitude of benefits that enhance our personal growth, relationships, and overall well-being.

- **Self-Confidence:** Assertiveness is intrinsically linked to self-confidence. When we assert ourselves, we send a powerful message to ourselves and others that our opinions and needs are valid and deserving of respect. Through assertiveness, we develop a strong sense of self-worth and belief in our abilities, empowering us to pursue our goals and aspirations with conviction.

- **Meeting Our Needs:** By being assertive, we actively communicate our needs and desires, ensuring they are met. Rather than remaining silent and resentful, we take charge of our lives and take the necessary steps to create the desired circumstances. Assertiveness allows us to ask for support, delegate tasks, and seek assistance when needed, leading to greater fulfillment and satisfaction in both personal and professional domains.

- **Conflict Resolution:** Passive behavior often leads to suppressed emotions and unresolved conflicts. By embracing assertiveness, we become more skilled in addressing conflicts directly and constructively. We respectfully express our concerns, perspectives, and boundaries, fostering open and honest communication. Through assertive conflict resolution, we promote understanding, find mutually beneficial solutions, and build stronger relationships based on trust and respect.

- **Reduced Stress:** Passivity can result in constant internal turmoil, as unexpressed thoughts and emotions weigh heavily on our minds and hearts. On the other hand, assertiveness relieves this burden by allowing us to voice our concerns and feelings authentically. By expressing ourselves assertively, we release stress, prevent resentment from building up, and create a healthier and more balanced emotional state.

- **Strengthened Relationships:** Assertiveness forms the foundation for healthy and meaningful relationships. When we assert ourselves, we establish clear boundaries, communicate openly, and foster mutual respect. Our assertiveness encourages others to treat us with consideration and appreciation. By demonstrating self-assuredness, we attract supportive and genuine connections while distancing ourselves from those who may seek to undermine our worth.

- **Improved Health:** The impact of assertiveness on our mental and physical health cannot be underestimated. We promote our well-being and cultivate a positive and fulfilling lifestyle through assertiveness. By expressing our needs and boundaries, we reduce the likelihood of being overwhelmed, overworked, or exploited. We prioritize self-care, establish a healthier work-life balance, and develop strategies to manage stress effectively.

As women, embracing assertiveness allows us to break free from the limitations imposed by passivity. It empowers us to own our voices, claim our space, and shape our destinies. By rejecting the idea that we must be passive and agreeable, we honor our worth, inspire others, and contribute to the collective movement of empowering women across the globe. Let us walk confidently in our assertiveness, embracing the many benefits awaiting us on this transformative journey.

## • 7 Ways To Become Empowered To Achieve

Let's start empowering ourselves to achieve greatness by following these invaluable tips:

1. **Develop a compelling vision and communicate it clearly.** Paint a vivid picture for others in your professional and personal life so they can see the vision and understand their role in it.

2. **Seek feedback and understand how others perceive you.** Embrace advice and input from supervisors, colleagues, and those you lead. Incorporate diverse perspectives into your decision-making process.

3. **Enhance your communication skills.** Take steps to improve your writing, speaking, and presentation abilities. Consider joining a speaker's bureau or taking communication classes to develop these vital skills.

4. **Be an active listener.** Prioritize listening over speaking and strive to understand others' thoughts and emotions. Engaging in meaningful conversations and asking questions helps foster a sense of shared purpose and encourages others to follow your lead.

5. **Cultivate a strong network and build political savvy.** Recognize that organizational politics exist, especially in larger companies. Develop professional diplomacy at all levels to become an influential and effective contributor.

6. **Thrive under stress.** Demonstrate patience, organization, and the ability to delegate tasks to prevent becoming overwhelmed. You inspire confidence in others by presenting yourself as calm, cool, and collected under pressure.

7. **Pay attention to your appearance.** Ensure that your attire is tailored, your grooming is impeccable, and you are culturally sensitive. By eliminating distractions, you can focus on conveying your message with impact.

By embracing these empowering strategies, you can unleash your full potential and pave the way for remarkable success.

## • 10 Ways To Become Empowered Through Self-Acceptance

Loulou Storey, a style and confidence coach, specializes in helping women revamp their appearance to cultivate self-assurance. Based on her sage and expert advice, here are some additional recommendations for enhancing confidence and executive presence.

1. **Embrace imperfection.** Grant yourself the grace to make mistakes and view them as opportunities for growth.

2. **Release self-criticism and view failure as a stepping stone** rather than an insurmountable barrier.

3. **Take action to bolster confidence.** Fearlessly pursue your great ideas and trust your intuition.

4. **Reject false humility.** Be transparent about your credentials and capabilities. Own your skills and avoid downplaying yourself.

5. **Explore uncharted territory.** Step outside your comfort zone and embrace new experiences.

6. **Advocate for yourself.** Refuse to accept blame when it's unwarranted, and confidently express your ideas.

7. **Harness the power of body language.** Walk, talk, and dress confidently, projecting your inner strength to others.

8. **Cultivate a supportive community of empowering individuals** who uplift and inspire you.

9. **Communicate your needs to others and delegate authority.** You don't have to shoulder everything alone.

10. **Lastly, prioritize self-love and patience** and recognize that your gifts, talents, skills, intelligence, and creativity hold immense value.

By applying these tips, you can harness and maintain your personal power. Standing up for yourself empowers you to shape how you present yourself to the world, ultimately fostering confidence and enhancing your executive presence.

# Benefits Of Having More Assertive Women In The Workforce

In today's rapidly evolving workplace, you as an assertive woman, are a crucial driver of positive change and a catalyst for transforming workforce dynamics. By embracing assertiveness, you can unlock many benefits that profoundly impact your career and the organization you work for. Let's delve into these benefits:

### *Effective Leadership*

Numerous studies consistently highlight the exceptional managerial prowess of assertive women. Their ability to confidently express themselves, set clear expectations, and provide constructive feedback fosters a positive work environment.

A shining example is unflappable Mary Barra, the CEO of General Motors since 2014. As the first woman to lead a major global automaker, Barra's assertiveness brought about transformative change within GM. Through her clear goal-setting, decisive choices, and accountability, she successfully guided the company through challenges, revitalizing its position in the industry. Barra's assertive management style fostered innovation, collaboration, and diversity, inspiring women in leadership roles. Her remarkable achievements demonstrate how strong women can make a significant impact as effective managers, steering the course of a company. In 2021, Time Magazine called her "an agent of change". This was her second time she was named on its Time100 annual list of the 100 most influential people in the world. For her innovation and leadership as the first woman to run a car company, Barra was also inducted into the 2023 Automotive Hall of Fame.

## Career Advancement

Assertiveness plays a vital role in propelling your career forward. When you assert yourself and confidently communicate your ideas, skills, and accomplishments, you gain recognition, trust, and opportunities for growth. Assertive women are more likely to be entrusted with important projects, receive promotions, and achieve their professional goals.

## Driving Innovation

Companies that prioritize gender diversity and create an environment where assertive women thrive reap the rewards of increased innovation. Assertive women bring fresh perspectives, challenge conventional thinking, and contribute diverse ideas. By embracing assertiveness, women drive creativity and problem-solving, ultimately enhancing the success of products, services, and overall business performance.

# Case Study — Eleanor Baum,

## pioneering female engineer

In the 1960s, NASA faced a unique challenge in safely returning astronauts from their space capsules. Eleanor Baum, a pioneering female engineer, led a team that developed the concept and design for the first parachute system used in the Mercury and Apollo space missions. NASA discovered that women approached problem-solving with a unique mindset and contributed valuable insights that played a crucial role in ensuring the safety of astronauts during reentry into the Earth's atmosphere.

This anecdote underscores the tangible benefits that women's involvement in the workforce brings, such as diverse perspectives, creativity, and problem-solving skills. It highlights the importance of inclusivity and the positive impact of women's participation in traditionally male-dominated sectors, demonstrating that diversity in the workforce leads to better outcomes and advancements.

By embracing assertiveness and fostering an environment that empowers women, we can collectively create workplaces that thrives on innovation, equality, and success.

## 5 Must Have Qualities To Get

# Further In Your Career

## *Self-Assurance*

A modern female employee should possess self-assurance by believing in her abilities and worth. Self-confidence allows for taking on challenges, speaking up, and asserting ideas with conviction.

## *Effective Communication*

Strong communication skills are vital for a modern female employee. Straightforward and assertive communication enables her to express thoughts, convey ideas persuasively, and engage in constructive dialogue, fostering collaboration and understanding.

## *Resilience*

Resilience is essential for navigating the dynamic and often demanding modern workplace. A confident and assertive female employee demonstrates resilience by bouncing back from setbacks, embracing challenges, and adapting to change with determination.

## *Emotional Intelligence*

Emotional intelligence is crucial in building strong relationships and effective teamwork. A modern female employee with emotional intelligence understands and manages her emotions while empathizing with others. This enables her to navigate conflicts assertively and build positive connections.

### *Assertive Decision-Making*

A confident and assertive female employee demonstrates the ability to make decisions independently. She considers various perspectives, weighs options, and takes decisive action, owning her choices and taking responsibility for outcomes.

By embodying these qualities, a modern female employee can navigate the professional landscape with confidence, assertiveness, and resilience, leading to personal growth, professional success, and positive contributions to the workplace.

### *Up Next?*

Get ready to discover the keys that unlock your true potential as a communicator, propelling you toward personal and professional triumphs.

# Chapter 3: Unveiling Your

# Default Communication Style

*"Your communication style is your*
*identity. It's your signature. It shapes*
*how you see the world, how the world*
*sees you, and how you relate."*

*- Susan Scott, author and speaker in the*
*field of leadership and communication*

Words can shape our world, and how we communicate can determine the course of our success. This next chapter delves into the intricate art of communication styles and how understanding and mastering them can open doors to meaningful connections, persuasive conversations, and empowered interactions.

*What does assertiveness genuinely look*
*like on you?*

Identifying your communication style might seem challenging, but it is the key to unlocking your potential. This book has touched on the nuances between passivity, assertiveness, and aggression. Now, it's time to get critical, examine how you naturally behave in various situations, and uncover your default communication style.

Within the realm of communication, there exist four distinct styles. While we may adapt to different types in different scenarios, we tend to gravitate towards one as our default. This becomes especially apparent when we feel uneasy or unprepared. Thus, recognizing your default style is crucial for creating positive change.

Imagine this scenario: You find yourself in a heated discussion at work, and without realizing it, your automatic response leans more toward aggression than assertiveness. Convinced that you're handling the situation flawlessly, you unintentionally come across as overbearing and dismissive, damaging your relationships and hindering collaboration. On the other hand, in another circumstance, you encounter discomfort, and your natural inclination is to withdraw, giving in to passivity. You may convince yourself that avoiding conflict is the best approach. Still, your opinions remain unheard, and your contributions go unnoticed.

In both cases, not being aware of your default communication style can lead to unintended consequences, affecting your interactions with colleagues and limiting your growth potential. Through self-assessment, you gain valuable insights into your communication patterns, empowering you to make intentional changes and develop a more effective and confident communication style that fosters meaningful connections and propels you toward success. Let's embark on this journey of self-discovery to transform your communication and assertiveness for the better.

Have a read over the following situations and answer candidly about which responses would best match your own:

**Scenario 1:** *Someone cuts in front of you as you queue to pay at the supermarket.*

Do you...

    A. Stay silent, feel discontented, and let them remain before you.
    B. Get angry and confront them, expressing annoyance with a sharp, "Hey jerk, no cuts!"
    C. Tap them on the shoulder and say, "Excuse me, but I was in the queue here first." You give them the benefit of the doubt, assuming they might not have seen you in line.

**Scenario 2:** *A co-worker who enjoys chatting wants to discuss a personal matter with you, but you're swamped with work and have no time to spare.*

How do you react?

    A. Let her talk for as long as she wants, knowing she needs someone to listen. You'll stay late to catch up on work.

B. Express frustration, feeling that she doesn't respect your schedule, and say, "I don't have all the time in the world, you know?!"

C. Listen for a minute or two, then kindly say, "I'm sorry you're going through a tough time, but right now, I must finish this presentation before the end of the day. Can we chat later, perhaps after work?"

Can you observe any patterns in your responses?

- If you answered A in both scenarios, your communication style tends to be **passive**.
- If you chose B, your default communication style is **aggressive**.
- If you responded with C, congratulations! You are **assertive** - the balanced approach between passivity and aggression.

You will encounter situations like those above – and many more significant ones every day. Each time, you must decide how to respond, and often, your reactions become automatic, reflecting your default communication style. That's why ensuring your default style is effective and empowering is crucial. I want it to be assertive, empowering you to express yourself confidently and achieve your desired outcomes.

Let me provide more examples of passive, aggressive, assertive, and passive-aggressive communication to help you identify where you fall on the assertiveness spectrum. Understanding the language and non-verbal cues associated with each style will enable you to assess your and others' natural communication preferences. You can gain valuable insights by delving into what these preferences reveal about your behavioral characteristics.

In addition, we'll explore how your communication might impact other people's feelings and subsequent reactions. This self-analysis will allow you to gauge your communication's effectiveness and identify improvement areas. Together, we'll strive to enhance your communication skills and foster positive interactions with others, benefiting both your personal and professional life.

# Gauging The Effectiveness Of The Four Communication Styles

## • The Assertive Style: The Holy Grail Of Effective Communication

In good communication, the assertive style stands tall as the Holy Grail. Here's how it looks in action:

Things An Assertive Communicator Is More Likely To Say:

- "I'm sorry, but I won't be able to help you this afternoon. I have a dentist's appointment."
- "Please, could you wind that window up? I'm feeling cold."
- "Please, could you turn the sound down? I'm struggling to concentrate."

When a woman speaks using terms like these, she confidently expresses her needs and boundaries while still being considerate of others.

## Assertive Behavioral Characteristics:

*Likely nonverbal indicators:*

- Open posture, relaxed, and no fidgeting.
- Makes good eye contact.
- The voice is at a medium pitch and volume.
- Gestures are even and expansive.
- Respects other people's personal space.

*Likely action indicators:*

- Achieve's goals without hurting others.
- Takes responsibility for choices made.
- Respects other people's rights while also being protective of your own.
- Able to accept compliments graciously.

- Asks directly for what you need while taking the possibility of rejection.

## How Assertiveness Makes Others Around You Feel:

- They can trust your words.
- They know where they stand with you.
- Respected by you, and they hold respect for you.
- Comfortable giving constructive criticism or compliments, as you can accept both.

## The End Result:

Assertive communication is the pinnacle of effective communication; embracing assertive behavioral characteristics can bring many empowering benefits to women.

When a woman communicates assertively through her nonverbal cues and gestures, she exudes confidence and self-assurance, commanding respect from others. Open posture, relaxed demeanor, and direct eye contact convey her strength and authenticity. Moreover, her voice's medium pitch and volume reinforce her assertiveness while maintaining respect for others.

In her actions, she achieves her goals without compromising the well-being of others, taking responsibility for her choices and respecting both her own rights and those of others. By gracefully accepting compliments and confidently expressing her needs, she navigates the world with poise and self-assuredness, fostering stronger relationships, advancing her career, and positively impacting those around her. Assertiveness empowers women to embrace their voices, seize opportunities, and shape their destinies with unwavering determination and grace.

## • The Aggressive Style: Bulldozing Your Way Through Life

The aggressive communication style can leave a trail of negative impacts on both the communicator and the recipients. Individuals with this style often resort to forceful and dominating language, demanding that others conform to their wishes without consideration for others' feelings.

Things An Aggressive Communicator Is More Likely To Say:

- "Listen up, you clueless bunch! It's my way or the highway, got it?"
- "What a cluster of incompetent jerks. I'm sick of having to clean up after your mess."
- "Can't you do anything right? I mean, it's like dealing with a horde of toddlers!"

- "Don't even get me started on your brilliant ideas; they're a joke!"
- "You must be out of your mind if you think that's good enough."
- "This is a disaster, and it's all your fault."
- "You better fix it, or else there will be consequences!"

Aggressive communicators often resort to name-calling, sarcasm, and blaming because they believe it gives them a false sense of power and control over others. They use these aggressive tactics to intimidate, belittle, and assert dominance, hoping to manipulate situations and force others into submission. However, this aggressive approach often leads to negative consequences, eroding trust, damaging relationships, and creating an environment of fear and hostility.

### Aggressive Behavioral Characteristics:

*Likely nonverbal indicators:*

- Use a loud voice.
- Make big sharp/threatening gestures.
- Invade your personal space, stand 'over you.'
- Scowl, glare, frown, or any other visual indication of unhappiness.
- Make 'bigger' postures than others.

*Likely action indicators:*

- Be frightening, threatening, or hostile.
- Be loud.

- Demand.
- Be belligerent and abrasive.
- Bully others.
- Be intimidating.
- Want to win at all costs, even at someone else's expense.

In short, this type of communicator believes their needs are the most important. It's as if they have more rights than anyone else. They will act as if they have more to contribute than others.

How Aggression Makes Others Around You Feel:

- Resentful.
- Hurt and/or afraid.
- Defensive, making them withdraw or fight back.
- Humiliated.
- Diminished respect for the aggressive person.

People on the receiving end of aggressive communication experience a range of emotions. They often feel compelled to fight back or withdraw, diminishing the chances of productive dialogue and understanding. Moreover, an aggressive communicator's message often gets lost in the delivery, as others are preoccupied with reacting to the aggressive manner rather than the content.

## Real-Life Experience Of An Aggressive Communicator

I once had a boss who fit the description of the most challenging person I'd ever worked with. He was undeniably brilliant and held a significant role in the company, but his lack of people skills was legendary. It was like walking on eggshells around him, as anything could set him off. Sometimes, it was over the tiniest details, and he expected us to read his mind, even when he frequently changed his mind. When things didn't go as he wanted, he'd explode.

His reactions were extreme – shouting, throwing things, using offensive language, and demanding that people be fired. I refused to carry out those demands, making me one of the rare few who confronted him directly. From the start, I clarified that I wouldn't tolerate such behavior toward me. It wasn't easy, and there were days when I wished to escape, but I stood my ground. Instead of reacting aggressively, I responded assertively; surprisingly, he began to respect that.

However, being around such aggression was utterly draining. It's no wonder others chose to avoid the man. Even though I stood up to him, the environment remained tense and uncomfortable. Aggressive behavior leaves scars on the workplace and relationships, making it harder for everyone to thrive and contribute effectively.

For those who think aggression will get them ahead, they may find momentary compliance. Still, it comes at a significant cost in the long run. A workplace filled with fear and hostility stifles creativity, collaboration, and productivity. Authentic leadership involves respect and support, not intimidation and fear. The damaging impact of aggressive communication was evident in every aspect of our work, and it's a lesson I'll never forget.

The End Result:

A communication style that fails to foster positive relationships leading to avoidance and resentment from others. Those who adopt this style may find themselves hitting a personal glass ceiling, hindering career growth due to unresolved people issues. It's crucial to recognize the negatives associated with aggression and work towards developing a more assertive communication style that promotes healthy and respectful interactions, unlocking opportunities for personal and professional growth.

## • The Passive Style: Head Down, Avoiding Conflict

Things A Passive Communicator Is More Likely To Say:

- 'I don't mind; you choose.'

- 'Oh, it doesn't matter/it's not important.'
- You can have it if you want it.'

Passive communicators may use these phrases to avoid conflict or prioritize others' preferences over their own. They often seek to please and accommodate others, even at the expense of their own needs and desires. This communication style may stem from a fear of confrontation or a desire to maintain harmony in relationships. Still, it can inadvertently lead to feelings of being overlooked or undervalued.

### Passive Behavioral Characteristics:

*Likely nonverbal indicators:*

- Speaks with a soft voice.
- Keeps their head down, making themselves as small as possible so they won't be noticed.
- Refuses eye contact.
- Fidgets.
- Demonstrates the outward signs of anxiety like restlessness, tension, sweating, shaking, etc.

*Likely action indicators:*

- Acts apologetically.
- Avoids conflict.
- Struggles to make decisions or take responsibility.
- Fails to stand up for their own rights or needs.

- Behaves as if other people's needs are more important.
- Yields to others.
- Blames others; she feels like a victim.
- Too uncomfortable to accept compliments.

## How Passivity Makes Others Around You Feel:

- Frustrated
- Empowered/Controlling
- Guilty
- Resentful
- Misunderstood
- Lack of Trust
- Compassion/Pity
- Uncomfortable

## The End Result:

The irony about passive communicators is that they spend all their time trying to please others and avoid conflict, but in the end, their low energy and victim mentality – often coupled with a reluctance to try new initiatives that could improve things – simply end up frustrating or even annoying people. Passive communication styles can be detrimental to personal growth and career advancement. By avoiding standing up for one's needs and downplaying their importance, a passive woman may find herself taken for granted and overlooked. In the long run, this style hinders progress and personal empowerment, leaving individuals feeling unfulfilled and disheartened.

## • The Passive-Aggressive Style: 'Cut Off Your Nose To Spite Your Face'

Passive-aggressive communication is a subtle yet harmful style where individuals express their negative feelings indirectly rather than addressing them openly. Instead of openly expressing their displeasure or dissatisfaction, passive-aggressive communicators may use sarcasm, backhanded compliments, or other covert means to convey their true feelings. They often appear agreeable on the surface but may resort to subtle acts of resistance, sabotage, or intentional inefficiency to express their underlying frustration or resentment. Passive-aggressive behavior can create confusion and tension in relationships and is often an unhealthy way of coping with conflict or unmet needs.

Things A Passive-Aggressive Communicator Is More Likely To Say:

- "It's fine; I'll just do everything myself since no one seems to care."
- "Wow, great job. I never would have thought to do it that way, but I guess it works."
- "I guess I'll just stay quiet since no one ever listens to me anyway."

- "Oh, I didn't realize you were too busy to help. I'll handle it all by myself, don't worry."
- "You're so lucky you can just say whatever you want without considering anyone else's feelings."
- "I'm sorry, I must have misunderstood. I'll keep my ideas to myself from now on."
- "If you think that's the best decision, who am I to argue? It's not like my opinion matters."

These phrases may seem innocent, but they carry passive-aggressive undertones that can convey hidden frustration, sarcasm, or resentment.

Passive-Aggressive Behavioral Characteristics:

*Likely nonverbal indicators:*

- Avoiding eye contact
- Sighing or heavy breathing
- Eye rolling
- Silent treatment

These nonverbal indicators can be subtle yet powerful in conveying hidden emotions and avoiding direct confrontation.

*Likely action indicators:*

- Be sarcastic.
- Sulk.
- Gossip.
- Complain/Whine.

- Manipulate
- Procrastinate
- Use backhanded compliments
- Indirectly express criticism
- Deliberate forgetfulness
- Sabotage
- Guilt-tripping
- Blaming others
- Indirectly seeking revenge

These actions and behaviors are characteristic of passive-aggressive communication, where the individual indirectly expresses their negative feelings, frustrations, or anger rather than addressing them directly.

## How Passive-Aggression Makes Others Around You Feel:

- Frustrated
- Confused
- Annoyed
- Guilty
- Powerless
- Hurt
- Distrustful
- Defensive
- Stressed
- Resentful

Overall, passive-aggressive communication can negatively impact relationships and create a tense and unhealthy atmosphere, as it prevents open and honest communication and leaves others feeling uneasy and uncertain.

The End Result:

Using a passive-aggressive communication style creates a breakdown in effective and healthy relationships. This style's indirect and subtle nature can lead to confusion, frustration, and resentment among those involved. Over time, it erodes trust and openness, hindering genuine communication and problem-solving. Passive-aggressive behavior often creates a cycle of negative emotions and responses, as others may become defensive or avoidant in response to the hidden tensions. Consequently, the real issues remain unresolved, and conflicts may escalate. Ultimately, this communication style hinders personal growth and prevents meaningful connections, leading to strained relationships and negatively impacting one's well-being and interpersonal interactions.

## Who Dares Wins?

To make understanding simple for how the four different communication styles work, let's look at who each style aims to "win" in typical situations.

**Assertive – I win, you win.**

An assertive person seeks a win-win outcome where both parties benefit.

**Aggressive – I win, you lose.**

Conversely, an aggressive communicator wants to win at any cost, often at the expense of others.

**Passive – I lose, you win.**

A submissive or passive individual may prioritize others' wins over their own.

**Passive-aggressive – I win, you lose.**

Lastly, the passive-aggressive style aims for a hidden victory, where they win while making others feel like they lose.

However, it's essential to note that these communication styles don't guarantee that these individuals always get what they want. For instance, walking away from an aggressive person rather than engaging in their competition can disrupt their plans and prevent them from achieving their desired outcome.

# Is Your Communication Style Hurting Your Career?

Unlock the potential of your career by delving into the realm of communication styles. As you embark on the journey of self-analysis to recognize your default communication style, there's another crucial aspect to explore: how your communication approach may impact your professional growth.

In this pursuit, be attentive to the tell-tale signs indicating your style requires some tender loving care. Let's uncover the nuances holding you back and pave the way for a more impactful and rewarding communication journey.

## • 5 Tell-Tale Signs Your Communication Style Is Affecting Your Professional Growth

1. **Nearly every encounter turns into an argument:** If you often find yourself in heated disagreements or conflicts that seem to escalate rather than resolve, it could indicate that your communication style needs adjustment.

Aggressive or passive-aggressive tendencies can be counterproductive and strain relationships.

2. **You feel like people don't listen or value your opinion:** Are you hesitant to voice your needs or preferences, opting to go along with others' decisions instead? A submissive communication style may keep you from asserting your ideas and desires, hindering your personal and professional growth.

3. **People respond poorly to your words and actions:** indicating a lack of assertiveness. Struggling to stand up for yourself or advocate for your opinions can signify a passive communication approach. If you frequently feel unheard or overlooked, working on assertiveness can empower you to make a more significant impact.

4. **People just don't seem to 'get' you:** Frequent misunderstandings or miscommunications with colleagues, friends, or family members might indicate that your communication style lacks clarity or is open to misinterpretation.

5. **You often think, "Who do they think they are talking to me like that!":** Avoiding feedback or becoming defensive when receiving constructive criticism can indicate sensitivity to communication issues. A willingness to accept

feedback and adapt accordingly is crucial for personal growth and improved communication.

Don't be disheartened if you've recognized that your communication style may be hindering your personal or professional growth!

Understanding and acknowledging areas for improvement is a decisive step toward positive change. Embrace this realization as an opportunity for growth and development. Remember, effective communication is a skill that can be honed with practice and determination. As you refine your communication style, you'll build stronger connections, increase your self-confidence, and create a more positive impact on those around you.

Stay committed to the journey of self-improvement, and don't give up! With persistence and a willingness to learn, you'll discover that enhancing your communication skills can lead to a more fulfilling and successful life. So, take this moment to empower yourself and embark on a transformative path toward becoming a more effective and confident communicator.

While you work on improving, remember this fundamental rule:

**The success of your communication is YOUR responsibility.**

If someone reacts differently than expected, take a moment to reflect on your own communication. Their response may be a result of something you said or implied. Avoid blaming others for communication mishaps; look within and take accountability for your part in it.

Likewise, if you face challenges with colleagues—lack of respect, poor responses, or adverse reactions—be willing to own your role. However, remember that people may have different communication styles, and introverts, for example, might not show immediate outward reactions.

The key is to ensure your communication conveys the intended message and elicits the desired response. Communication goes beyond mere words; it includes body language, gestures, and expressions. Our communication style reflects our self-perception and views of others, influencing our leadership and management abilities.

## *Up Next?*

In the next chapter, we reveal the intricate link between communication styles and the unique challenges women face in embracing powerful, authoritative, and assertive communication. We'll explore societal factors, cultural conditioning, and unconscious biases that might hinder women from expressing their true potential naturally. Join me as I unveil the barriers and unveil strategies to empower women in conquering the communication landscape, forging a path to unapologetically assertive and impactful communication.

# Chapter 4: Beware Of

# Communication Traps

*To be passive is to let others decide for you. To be aggressive is to decide for others. To be assertive is to decide for yourself. And to trust that there is enough, that you are enough.*

*–Edith Eva Eger, Holocaust Survivor and Therapist*

In this chapter, I'll help you delve into the factors contributing to the confidence deficit hindering you from embracing assertiveness and unlocking your full potential. The confidence gap is a complex interplay of various elements. Understanding them is crucial to breaking free from self-limiting beliefs and empowering ourselves as communicators.

Confidence is essential for executive presence, and a lack of personal confidence is one of the most significant barriers to assertiveness. According to writers Katie Kay and Claire Shipman, confidence holds more value than competence.

However, the confidence gap is a well-documented phenomenon highlighting the disparity between men and women concerning self-assurance and self-belief. Numerous studies have shown that women underestimate their abilities, hesitate to take on new challenges, and are less likely to negotiate for what they deserve. This gap often leaves women feeling less confident and reluctant to assert themselves, significantly impacting their personal and professional growth.

# Obstacles Exacerbating The Confidence Gap

The following are some of the obstacles that women alone face, further exacerbating the gap in confidence between men and women:

## • The Superwoman Syndrome

Societal expectations and gender norms significantly shape women's self-perceptions and roles. Balancing work and social responsibilities can lead to internal conflict and doubts about handling multiple roles, affecting confidence and assertiveness. The persistent "superwoman" ideal places unrealistic pressure on women to excel in various positions, damaging self-esteem.

While progress has been made, women face burdensome choices between careers, relationships, and family responsibilities. The notion of the "superwoman" still prevails, where women are expected to effortlessly manage various roles, from being a dedicated professional to a caring wife, mother, and more. Unrealistic media representations and social media pressures add to this burden, setting unattainable standards detrimental to women's self-esteem and sense of self-worth.

Breaking free from these constraints and embracing genuine confidence is essential for personal and professional growth. By challenging norms, cultivating self-worth, and uplifting other women, you can shatter the confidence gap and empower yourself and others as strong, authentic leaders.

### Communication Tip

Embrace your vulnerability and seek support. To overcome the pressure of the "superwoman" syndrome and cultivate genuine confidence, embracing vulnerability and seeking help from your peers and communities is crucial. Opening up about the challenges of balancing multiple roles and expressing self-doubt can create a safe space for dialogue and understanding. Together, women can uplift and empower one another, breaking free from unrealistic expectations and fostering an environment of genuine confidence and assertiveness. Remember, it's okay to ask for support and lean on others—it's a sign of strength, not weakness.

## • Believing In "Female Only" Personality Traits

Women, like men, exhibit a diverse range of personality traits. However, societal stereotypes and cultural conditioning may lead women to believe that specific characteristics are inherently masculine or feminine. As a result, some women may struggle to embrace assertiveness because they fear deviating from societal expectations. The belief that personality traits are set in stone can limit personal growth and prevent women from discovering their full potential.

Could your belief in the following 'female only' personality traits limit your confidence and affect your communication?

### *Perfectionism*

Do you exhibit perfectionist tendencies? Do you have unrealistically high standards for yourself? Then this could lead to self-doubt and a fear of making mistakes.

Constantly pursuing flawlessness can erode confidence by feeling you will never meet your expectations.

## Self-Criticism

If you engage in self-critical behavior, you may excessively focus on your perceived flaws and shortcomings. Constant self-criticism can undermine self-confidence and make it challenging for you to recognize and appreciate your strengths and achievements.

## Fear of failure

If you have an intense fear of failure, you may hesitate to take risks or pursue new opportunities. Negative past experiences, such as rejections, criticism, or failure, can impact women's confidence levels. These experiences may create a fear of failure and a reluctance to put yourself in challenging situations. Over time, this fear can inhibit your assertiveness as you become wary of taking risks and seeking growth opportunities. The fear of failing or making a mistake can hold you back from stepping outside your comfort zones and trying new things.

## People-Pleasing

Women are often expected to be accommodating and nurturing, making it challenging for some to say no when they feel overwhelmed or need to prioritize their needs. The inability to assert boundaries and say no can lead to feelings of powerlessness and undermine self-confidence.

Do you have a solid inclination to please others? Do you prioritize the needs and desires of others over your own? This people-pleasing behavior can lead to a lack of assertiveness, as you may avoid asserting your opinions or boundaries to prevent conflict or disapproval.

It's essential to recognize that assertiveness and confidence are not fixed traits but skills that can be learned and developed over time. By understanding the factors contributing to the confidence deficit, you can begin to challenge self-limiting beliefs and embrace a more empowered communication style.

## • Stereotyping Of Women & Gender Bias

Stereotypes about women's roles and capabilities persist in various cultures and societies. We are often boxed into traditional roles and deemed less capable in specific domains, perpetuating gender bias. Overcoming these stereotypes requires challenging societal norms, promoting gender equality, and actively debunking misconceptions about our abilities.

**Communication Tip**

We can counteract gender bias by confidently asserting our expertise and accomplishments in professional settings. Emphasizing achievements and contributions will help dispel preconceptions and showcase competence.

## • Gender Bias Backlash

When demonstrating assertiveness and leadership qualities, we may face backlash from both men and women who find these behaviors at odds with societal expectations. This backlash can manifest as criticism, resistance, or attempts to undermine authority.

**Communication Tip**

Embracing assertiveness while remaining empathetic and approachable can help us to navigate gender bias backlash. Building solid connections through open communication and active listening can foster understanding and break down barriers.

# • The Double Bind: Women's Balancing Act - Competence Vs. Likability

Assertiveness for women can be a tightrope walk, where they must balance being seen as competent leaders while still being likable. Research reveals that assertive behavior is sometimes misinterpreted as "bossy" or "aggressive" when displayed by women, affecting how likable they are perceived to be.

A notable example of this struggle is evident in the political arena. During her presidential campaigns, Hillary Clinton faced the challenge of being assertive while also managing the likability factor. Criticized for being too assertive and lacking warmth, she encountered the classic double bind many women face in leadership roles.

This double bind and likability factor have also impacted Greta Thunberg, the Swedish climate activist. Despite her young age, Greta fearlessly advocates for urgent climate action. Yet, she faced criticism and dismissive remarks from some prominent figures during her powerful speeches at international forums and the United Nations.

In response to her passionate and assertive calls for climate action, Greta was ridiculed and belittled by those who perceived her assertiveness as "over-emotional" or "hysterical." Such derogatory comments often stem from gender-based assumptions and stereotypes, seeking to undermine the credibility of her activism by invalidating her assertive communication style.

Greta Thunberg's experiences exemplify assertive and outspoken women's challenges, especially when addressing critical global issues. Despite facing such gender bias, her resilience and determination inspired many worldwide. Her journey emphasizes the urgent need to manage and confront gender bias in society, ensuring women's voices and communication styles are respected and valued in all areas.

**Communication Tip**

To navigate the double bind effectively, you can emphasize collaborative and inclusive leadership styles. Building rapport and trust with colleagues can positively influence perceptions and create a more supportive environment for assertiveness.

# Is Your Communication Still Style Holding You Back?

As we discussed in the previous chapter, your communication style speaks volumes about you - how you interact with others and how you value yourself. It can exude confidence or make you appear shy and hesitant. Mastering effective communication is essential in all aspects of life, yet it can be challenging, especially for women.

Finding the right communication balance can feel like a tightrope walk for a woman. If you're assertive, you risk being labeled as a "bitch," but being passive opens you up to being taken advantage of. Striking that middle ground can still feel inadequate, with various factors at play, especially in the workplace.

Stereotypes surrounding women are common but insidious. Despite doing the same as men, women often face harsher judgments and criticism for assertiveness. Being passive isn't the solution either, as it holds you back from reaching your potential.

Asserting yourself doesn't mean being aggressive; it's about expressing your ideas confidently and listening to others. Proving yourself in a male-dominated world may be challenging, but women have made remarkable progress. However, it's crucial to communicate without aggression or passivity, avoiding anger-driven outbursts that can undermine your credibility.

Communicating effectively, even amid disagreements, is essential for growth and success. Building strong communication bridges fosters understanding and respect, ultimately paving the way for advancement.

# • The Impact Of Emotional Intelligence On Communication

In the workplace, communication is assessed using emotional intelligence (E.Q.),which measures how emotions influence our thinking and interactions. Emotionally intelligent individuals are attuned to their own feelings and those of others, enabling them to navigate social situations and communication effectively.

Being too low or too high on the E.Q. scale can affect how you communicate. Reacting emotionally or getting easily upset may be perceived as a weakness, hindering your ability to achieve your goals. Conversely, suppressing emotions and being unaware of others' feelings can lead to judgment and isolation. The key is striking a balance and communicating without excessive emotions. Assert yourself firmly, avoid aggression, and carefully consider your responses. Instead of shouting in anger, express your feelings and be open to dialogue.

As you practice communication, you'll discover the ideal balance and build confidence in being more assertive. This will help you overcome the obstacles and issues discussed in this chapter that might currently hold you back.

## *Up Next?*

Welcome to the thrilling second part of our journey! In the upcoming power-packed chapter, we unlock the immense potential of your mindset, revealing how it holds the key to conquering obstacles, defying self-doubt, and unleashing the fearless, assertive woman within. Prepare to embark on a transformative quest, where we equip you with the tried-and-true strategies to soar confidently and break free from limitations. It's time to embrace the unstoppable force you are and claim the success and empowerment you deserve! Are you prepared to take charge of your destiny and become the confident, assertive woman you've always envisioned? Let's dive in and make it happen!

# Part 2 — Investing In Your Self: Unleashing Confidence & Assertiveness Strategies For Women On The Path To Leadership

# Chapter 5: Unleashing the Leader Within – Embrace Your Distinctive Mindset!

Are you ready to embark on a life-changing voyage that will redefine how you lead and achieve? In this chapter, we'll dive deep into the dynamic world of female leadership, exploring the extraordinary power of mindset. Discover how positivity, mindfulness, and mental resilience can elevate you to new heights of confidence and assertiveness.

You'll find inspiration in real-life examples, including the awe-inspiring journey of Indra Nooyi, former CEO of PepsiCo. Unleash the trailblazer within you and set a path where success knows no bounds. Get ready to revolutionize your approach to leadership and leave an indelible mark on the world. The time has come to embrace your true potential and lead with brilliance!

## Developing A Distinctive Leadership Mindset

In your pursuit of leadership excellence, developing a robust and purposeful mindset will become your indispensable asset, not just an advantage. As a woman striving to achieve your goals, you may face unique challenges and obstacles, but with the right mindset, you can stand out from the crowd; thinking inside the box will not bring new and exciting ideas. Beyond skills and qualifications, a leadership mindset shapes how you perceive challenges, approach decisions, and inspire those around you. Embracing this mindset empowers you to unleash your full potential, foster resilience in adversity, and drive change. It becomes the foundation upon which great leaders build their vision, navigate complexities, and shape a better future.

As you cultivate a leadership mindset, you unlock many benefits beyond professional success, transcend into personal growth, fulfill aspirations, and create a lasting legacy. In this section, we'll explore the distinctive mindset traits that pave the way for women in leadership. By understanding how each intertwines, you'll harness a transformative force capable of overcoming obstacles, seizing opportunities, and leaving an indelible mark on the world.

# A Journey Into Growth Mindset

Now, let's delve deeper into the power of a growth mindset – a mindset that embraces challenges, values effort and learning, and fosters resilience. This mindset is a great place to start when developing a distinctive leadership mindset. A growth mindset enables you to perceive setbacks as stepping stones, obstacles as opportunities, and failures as invaluable lessons. It opens doors to continuous growth and propels you towards achieving your boldest aspirations.

## *5 Ways To Cultivate A Growth Mindset Today*

1. **Embrace challenges:** Instead of shying away from challenges, embrace them as opportunities to learn and grow. Welcome new experiences that push you beyond your comfort zone, whether taking on a new project at work or pursuing a hobby you've always wanted to try.

2. **View effort as the path to mastery:** Understand that effort and hard work are essential ingredients in the journey towards mastery. See mistakes and setbacks as valuable learning experiences that propel you forward rather than signs of failure.

3. **Learn from feedback:** Embrace positive and constructive feedback as valuable insights that can help you improve. Be open to receiving

feedback from others and use it to refine your skills and approaches.

4. **Cultivate a love for learning:** Cultivate curiosity and thirst for knowledge. Engage in continuous learning by seeking new information, attending workshops, or reading books that expand your horizons.

5. **Surround yourself with growth-minded individuals:** Surround yourself with people who value growth and development. Share your aspirations with supportive peers, mentors, or coaches who can encourage and challenge you to reach new heights.

By incorporating these practices into your daily life, you'll gradually embrace the power of a growth mindset. Remember, adaption begins with a single step, and every effort you make to foster a growth mindset will propel you toward becoming an extraordinary leader.

# The Power Of Positive Thinking

Positive thinking is a formidable companion to your growth mindset. It enables you to see the world through a lens of optimism and hope, promoting a mindset that believes in possibilities and solutions rather than dwelling on problems. Embracing positive thinking allows you to maintain a sense of confidence and resilience even in the face of challenges, making it an invaluable tool in your pursuit of a distinctive female leadership style.

### *Benefits Of Positive Thinking:*

- **Resilience in adversity:** Positive thinking equips you with the mental fortitude to bounce back from setbacks and challenges. It allows you to approach obstacles with a can-do attitude, fostering the belief that you can overcome adversity.

- **Improved decision-making:** A positive mindset clears away self-doubt and negative self-talk, enabling you to make decisions with greater clarity and confidence. This leads to more effective problem-solving and creative thinking.

- **Motivation and goal achievement:** A positive outlook makes you more likely to stay motivated and committed to your goals. Positive thinking fuels determination and perseverance, propelling you forward on your leadership journey.

- **Enhanced emotional well-being:** Positive thinking improves well-being, reducing stress and anxiety. It fosters a sense of inner peace and contentment, allowing you to maintain balance amidst life's challenges.

- **Inspirational leadership:** As a leader, positive thinking inspires and uplifts those around you. It creates a supportive and encouraging environment where others feel empowered to excel and contribute their best.

### *Ways To Foster Positive Thinking*

Practice Gratitude

Start each day by acknowledging the things you are grateful for. Gratitude shifts your focus to the positive aspects of life and amplifies feelings of contentment and joy. Here are a few brief ways you can practice gratitude:

- *Gratitude journal:* Dedicate a few minutes each morning or evening to write down three things you are grateful for. It could be simple joys like a warm cup of coffee, a supportive friend, or a beautiful sunrise. Reflecting on these blessings will infuse your day with positivity.

- *Gratitude in challenging times:* Even during difficult moments, strive to find something to be grateful for. This might be the strength to overcome a challenge, the support of loved ones, or the opportunity to learn and grow. Acknowledging these silver linings can empower you to navigate adversity with resilience.

- *Gratitude affirmations:* **Create daily affirmations that focus on gratitude. Repeat these affirmations throughout the day to reinforce a positive mindset. For example, say, "I am grateful for the abundance in my life" or "I am thankful for the opportunities that come my way."**

As you incorporate these gratitude practices into your daily routine, you will discover a profound shift in your outlook on life. Embracing gratitude will enhance your leadership journey and amplify your capacity to lead with brilliance and compassion.

## Encourage Optimism

Develop a more optimistic mindset by consciously reframing negative thoughts into positive ones. Here are a few ways to foster optimism:

- *Positive reframing:* **When facing challenges, train yourself to view setbacks as opportunities for growth. Instead of dwelling on what went wrong, focus on the lessons learned and the potential for future success.**

- *Surround yourself with positivity:* **Surround yourself with positive and supportive individuals who uplift and encourage you. Engage in** conversations that inspire optimism and avoid excessive exposure to negativity.

- *Visualize success:* Envision yourself achieving your goals and visualize the positive outcomes of your efforts. This visualization technique can boost confidence and motivation to strive for success.

- *Celebrate small wins:* Acknowledge and celebrate your achievements, no matter how small they may seem. Recognizing your progress fuels a sense of accomplishment and reinforces a positive mindset.

- *Practice self-compassion:* Be kind to yourself and avoid self-criticism. Treat yourself with the same compassion and understanding you would offer a friend facing challenges.

Adopting a more optimistic outlook will boost your well-being and positively impact those around you. Your optimism will be contagious, inspiring others to approach challenges with renewed hope and resilience.

## Focus On Solutions

Instead of fixating on problems, direct your energy towards finding solutions. Here's how you can shift your focus:

- *Identify the core issue:* Clearly define the problem and its root causes. Understanding the core issue will guide you toward practical solutions.

- *Brainstorm alternatives:* Engage in creative brainstorming to generate multiple potential solutions. Encourage diverse perspectives and explore innovative ideas.

- *Break tasks into manageable steps:* When facing complex challenges, break them down into smaller, achievable steps. Tackling one step at a time will prevent becoming overwhelmed and foster a sense of progress.

- *Seek guidance and collaboration:* Don't hesitate to seek input from colleagues, mentors, or experts. Collaborative problem-solving can lead to more comprehensive and effective solutions.

- *Learn from past experiences:* Reflect on past experiences and lessons learned. Apply insights from previous challenges to inform your approach to current issues.

By adopting a solution-focused mindset, you become an empowered leader capable of navigating obstacles with resilience and creativity. Your ability to find solutions will inspire confidence in your team and foster a culture of proactive problem-solving.

## Practice Positive Self-Affirmations

Embrace positive self-affirmations to boost self-confidence and combat self-doubt. Here are some tips for incorporating them into your daily routine:

- *Identify your strengths:* Recognize and acknowledge your unique strengths and capabilities. Use these strengths as the foundation for your affirmations.

- *Create personalized affirmations:* Craft positive statements reflecting your goals and aspirations. Make them personal, meaningful, and in the present tense.

- *Repeat affirmations regularly:* Set aside time each day to repeat your affirmations, silently or aloud. Consistent repetition reinforces positive beliefs about yourself.

- *Visualize your success:* As you recite affirmations, visualize yourself achieving your goals and embodying the qualities you wish to strengthen.

- *Believe in yourself:* Embrace your affirmations with an unwavering belief in your abilities. Trust that you are capable of achieving what you set your mind to.

Positive self-affirmations can transform your self-perception, helping you embrace your leadership strengths and values. As you affirm your worth, you radiate confidence and authenticity, inspiring others to recognize their potential.

## Practice Mindful Awareness

Cultivate mindfulness to heighten self-awareness and stay present in the moment. Mindfulness practices include:

- *Mindful breathing:* Focus on your breath for a few moments each day. Pay attention to the sensation of each inhale and exhale, grounding yourself in the present moment.

- *Mindful observation:* Engage your senses to observe your surroundings without judgment. Notice the sights, sounds, and sensations around you.

- *Mindful listening:* When engaged in conversations, listen attentively to the speaker without interrupting or formulating responses in your mind. Truly be present in the exchange.

- *Mindful pause:* Before reacting to stressful situations, take a moment to pause and collect your thoughts. Mindful pauses help you respond thoughtfully rather than react impulsively.

- *Mindful reflection:* Set aside time to reflect on your thoughts and emotions. Allow yourself to process experiences without attachment or judgment.

Practicing mindfulness enhances your ability to lead with clarity and emotional intelligence. By being fully present in your interactions, you foster genuine connections and better understand the needs and perspectives of those around you.

As you merge the power of a growth mindset with the force of positive thinking, you will witness a transformative shift in your leadership capabilities. Embrace the belief that you are destined for greatness, and with this foundation, you will lead with brilliance and inspire others to do the same. The time is now to unlock the full potential of your distinctive leadership mindset and trailblaze a path of success, impact, and fulfillment.

## Case Study — Indra Nooyi, Former CEO Of Pepsico

The inspiring journey of Indra Nooyi, the former CEO of PepsiCo, is a fantastic example for us to look at. Notably, her power of mindset was pivotal in her exceptional leadership and accomplishments.

Indra Nooyi, a trailblazing businesswoman, served as the CEO of PepsiCo from 2006 to 2018, making her one of the most influential female leaders in the world. Throughout her tenure, she demonstrated unwavering determination and a positive mindset that propelled her and the company to new heights.

Nooyi faced numerous challenges and biases as a woman of color in the predominantly male-dominated corporate world. However, she embraced these hurdles as opportunities to prove her capabilities rather than allowing them to hold her back.

Nooyi's belief in the power of positive thinking and mindfulness was evident in her approach to leadership. She consistently emphasized the importance of adapting to change and seeing every situation, even setbacks, as an occasion to learn and grow. This mindset enabled her to weather challenges and inspired her team to adopt a similar outlook.

Under Nooyi's leadership, PepsiCo saw remarkable growth and transformation. She steered the company toward healthier product offerings and sustainability initiatives, recognizing the importance of aligning business strategies with societal needs. Her vision for the company's future emphasized long-term sustainability and ethical practices.

Additionally, Nooyi was known for her focus on empowering employees and fostering a culture of inclusivity. She valued diverse perspectives and actively sought input from team members at all levels. By creating an environment where individuals felt valued and heard, she unleashed the full potential of PepsiCo's workforce.

Nooyi's extraordinary journey and achievements highlight the profound impact of a positive mindset in leadership. Her resilience, adaptability, and commitment to embracing challenges exemplify how a strong belief in one's abilities can pave the way for success, even in the face of adversity. By nurturing a growth-oriented mindset, Nooyi shattered glass ceilings and left a lasting legacy as a true inspiration for aspiring female leaders worldwide.

# Building Mental Resilience: Thriving In The Face Of Challenges

As you develop a distinctive leadership mindset, your two most potent allies will be a growth mindset and positive thinking. These intertwined elements form the bedrock upon which mental resilience thrives, creating a powerful force capable of propelling you forward in your leadership endeavors.

Mental resilience is the extraordinary ability to navigate life's inevitable challenges with grace and strength. As a female leader, cultivating mental resilience empowers you to bounce back from setbacks, adapt to change, and maintain focus and determination amidst adversity. This indispensable quality lets you stay composed and solution-oriented, even when faced with daunting obstacles.

When you develop mental resilience, you become better equipped to embrace change as an opportunity for growth and transformation. Rather than succumbing to self-doubt or despair, you harness the power of resilience to emerge stronger and wiser from life's trials. With mental strength, you can confidently navigate the uncertainties of leadership, inspire others to do the same and transform challenges into stepping stones toward success. Embracing mental resilience sets you on a path to thrive as a leader, making you unstoppable in achieving your goals and fulfilling your vision.

# • Examples Of Female-Oriented Mental Resilience And How To Achieve Them

### *Bouncing Back From Setbacks Like Sheryl Sandberg*

As the COO of Facebook, Sheryl Sandberg faced personal and professional challenges, including the sudden loss of her husband. Despite the heartbreak, she demonstrated remarkable mental resilience by channeling her grief into a powerful message of strength and support for others. To achieve this level of mental resilience, practice acknowledging and accepting your emotions while seeking support from loved ones. Focus on building a growth mindset by viewing challenges as opportunities for learning and growth.

How to practice acknowledging and accepting your emotions:

- *Allow yourself to feel:* When setbacks occur, give yourself permission to experience a range of emotions, including sadness, frustration, or anger. Avoid suppressing emotions, as this can hinder the healing process.

- *Name your emotions:* Identifying and labeling your feelings can help you understand them better and gain control over their impact.

- *Journaling:* Write down your emotions and thoughts to process your feelings and gain perspective on the situation.

- *Mindfulness:* Engage in mindfulness practices, such as meditation or deep breathing, to stay present with your emotions and avoid getting overwhelmed.

Ways to seek support from loved ones:

- *Reach out to family and friends:* Share your experiences with people you trust, as talking openly about your challenges can provide emotional support and reassurance.

- *Join support groups:* Seek out communities or support groups where individuals are experiencing similar setbacks. Connecting with others can offer a sense of belonging and encouragement.

- *Seek professional help if needed:* If you find it challenging to cope with setbacks, consider seeking help from a therapist or counselor who can provide guidance and additional coping strategies.

### Navigating Gender Bias Like Melinda Gates

Melinda Gates, co-chair of the Bill & Melinda Gates Foundation, has been a vocal advocate for gender equality. Despite facing gender bias and societal expectations, she remains steadfast in her commitment to empowering women globally. To emulate her mental resilience, develop strong self-worth, and surround yourself with a supportive network. Practice positive thinking by countering negative thoughts with affirmations of your worth and capabilities.

How to develop a strong sense of self-worth:

- *Reflect on your accomplishments:* Take time to recognize and celebrate your achievements, big and small. Acknowledging your capabilities boosts self-confidence.

- *Embrace self-compassion:* Treat yourself with the kindness and understanding you would offer a friend. Avoid self-criticism and practice self-acceptance.

- *Challenge negative self-talk:* When faced with self-doubt, challenge negative thoughts by replacing them with positive affirmations. Remind yourself of your strengths and skills.

- *Set clear boundaries:* Prioritize your well-being by setting boundaries in personal and professional relationships. Assert yourself when necessary to protect your time and energy.

Ways to build a supportive network:

- *Seek out like-minded individuals:* Connect with women and allies who share your values and goals. Networking with supportive individuals can provide encouragement and motivation.

- *Join women's leadership groups:* Participate in women-focused leadership organizations or forums to foster mentorship, guidance, and camaraderie.

- *Cultivate diverse connections:* Build relationships with individuals from different backgrounds and industries to gain diverse perspectives and insights.

- *Be a supportive ally:* Actively support and uplift other women in your network. Being a part of a community that empowers one another creates a more resilient support system.

### *Overcoming Imposter Syndrome Like Michelle Obama*

Even as the First Lady of the United States, Michelle Obama has openly discussed her struggles with imposter syndrome—a feeling of not deserving one's success. She tackled this challenge head-on by focusing on her achievements and reminding herself of her value. To conquer imposter syndrome, celebrate your successes and acknowledge your contributions.

Cultivate a growth mindset by seeing yourself as a work in progress, constantly learning and evolving.

Ways to challenge feeling like an imposter:

- *Record your achievements:* Keep a journal or a list of your accomplishments, both big and small. When feelings of self-doubt arise, review this record to remind yourself of your progress.

- *Talk to supportive individuals:* Share your feelings with trusted friends, mentors, or colleagues who can provide reassurance and perspective. They can offer insights into your strengths and help dispel self-doubt.

- *Challenge negative thoughts:* Identify and challenge the negative thoughts that fuel imposter syndrome. Replace them with positive affirmations and realistic self-appraisals.

- *Accept constructive feedback:* Embrace feedback as an opportunity for growth rather than evidence of inadequacy. Recognize that everyone makes mistakes and that improvement is a natural part of learning.

- *Celebrate your progress:* Acknowledge your journey and the effort you put into reaching your goals. Treat yourself with kindness and patience, understanding that self-development is continuous.

## Handling Workplace Pressures Like Oprah Winfrey

Oprah Winfrey, the media mogul, and philanthropist, has faced numerous challenges in her career. Through it all, she has exhibited mental resilience by maintaining a positive outlook and staying true to her vision. To mirror this resilience, practice gratitude daily by writing down things you are thankful for. Embrace positive thinking by visualizing your success and repeating empowering affirmations.

Ways to overcome common workplace pressures:

- *Time management:* Prioritize tasks and set realistic deadlines to avoid feeling overwhelmed. Break larger projects into smaller, manageable steps, and tackle them individually.

- *Delegate and seek support:* Don't be afraid to delegate tasks when appropriate and seek support from colleagues or supervisors when needed. Collaboration can lighten the burden and provide fresh perspectives.

- *Create a supportive environment:* Foster a positive and supportive work environment by establishing open communication and respectful relationships with coworkers. Share your challenges and seek advice from trusted colleagues.

- *Practice mindfulness and breathing exercises:* Incorporate mindfulness and deep-breathing exercises into your daily routine to reduce stress and increase focus. Take short breaks during hectic periods to clear your mind.

- *Set boundaries:* Know your limits and set boundaries to maintain a healthy work-life balance. Avoid taking on excessive tasks or working overtime regularly, leading to burnout.

- *Celebrate small wins:* Acknowledge and celebrate your achievements, no matter how small. Recognizing your progress can boost morale and provide motivation during challenging times.

- *Seek professional development:* Invest in ongoing professional development to enhance your skills and build confidence in your abilities. Expanding your knowledge can help you feel more equipped to handle workplace pressures.

### Embracing Change Like Ginni Rometty

Ginni Rometty, a former CEO of IBM, navigated the company through significant technological change. Her mental resilience was evident in her ability to confidently adapt and lead. To cultivate similar strengths, welcome change as an opportunity for growth. Develop a growth mindset by seeking new challenges and embracing a learning-oriented approach to leadership.

How to adapt to change with confidence:

- *Stay curious:* **Approach** change with curiosity, seeking to understand the reasons behind it and the potential benefits it can bring. Ask questions and stay informed about the changes happening in your industry or organization.

- *Flexibility and adaptability:* **Be** flexible in your thinking and actions. Embrace the idea that change is constant, and the ability to adjust and pivot will serve you well in navigating new situations.

- *Self-reflection:* Take time for self-reflection during times of change. Assess your strengths and areas for improvement, and identify how you can leverage your skills to thrive in the changing environment.

- *Focus on solutions:* **Instead** of dwelling on challenges, focus on finding solutions. Look for opportunities to contribute positively to the changes and offer constructive ideas to improve processes.

- *Positive self-talk:* Monitor your inner dialogue and replace negative self-talk with positive affirmations. Remind yourself of your past successes and your resilience in the face of change.

- *Take calculated risks:* Embrace calculated risks and step out of your comfort zone. Sometimes, taking a chance at new opportunities can lead to remarkable growth and advancement.

- *Continuous learning:* Embrace a mindset of constant learning. Seek resources, workshops, or courses that can help you acquire new skills and knowledge related to the changes around you.

Drawing inspiration from these remarkable women and integrating their practices into your life, you can cultivate your mental resilience and flourish as a female leader. Remember, mental resilience is not a fixed trait but a skill that can be honed with practice and perseverance. Embrace the journey of building mental resilience alongside your growth mindset and positive thinking, and witness its tremendous impact on your leadership journey.

## *Up Next?*

As we reach the culmination of this chapter, you should have begun the rewarding journey into developing a distinctive mindset that sets you on the path of leadership excellence. Embracing a growth mindset, practicing positive thinking, and nurturing mental resilience have become your powerful allies, empowering you to conquer challenges and embrace change with unwavering confidence.

In the upcoming chapter, we delve into the awe-inspiring realm of your innate qualities as a woman. Unlocking the true power of your womanhood, we'll explore how these exceptional attributes can set you apart in your personal and professional life. Prepare to discover the boundless possibilities of being a woman in leadership as I unveil the key strategies to unleash your full potential and pave the way for you to emerge as an empowered, confident, and influential leader.

# Chapter 6: Unleash Your Inherent Power: Embrace Your Womanhood & Reach Your Full Potential

You are truly extraordinary! As a woman, you possess unique strengths and qualities that set you apart as a remarkable trailblazer and leader. Embrace these qualities and unlock your potential by developing emotional intelligence—an essential aspect of becoming a more confident and assertive female leader. Let's explore why emotional intelligence is a superpower for women on their journey to leadership excellence.

# Emotional Intelligence: Your Superpower For Leadership

As a woman, you have an inherent emotional intelligence (EI) advantage. EI encompasses recognizing, understanding, and managing your emotions, as well as the feelings of others. Research consistently shows that women score higher in EI than men, making it an integral part of your leadership toolkit.

## The Female Advantage In Emotional Intelligence

Women have higher levels of empathy, emotional sensitivity, and interpersonal understanding. This allows you to form strong connections with your team members, fostering open communication and a supportive work environment. Your heightened ability to read and respond to emotions enables you to navigate complex interpersonal dynamics with finesse, enhancing collaboration and consensus-building within your organization.

## Embracing The Politics Of Empathy

Your capacity for empathy is a powerful tool for nurturing relationships and driving team cohesion. Demonstrating genuine empathy creates a sense of psychological safety within your team, encouraging open expression of ideas and concerns. As a leader, you can use the "politics of empathy" to create an inclusive environment where every voice is heard, inspiring team members to contribute their best and feel valued.

### The Role Of Self-Confidence In Emotional Intelligence

Believing in yourself and your abilities is vital to honing emotional intelligence. A healthy level of self-confidence allows you to navigate challenging situations gracefully and with poise as you trust your intuition and decision-making skills. When you lead with self-assurance, you inspire confidence in others and set a positive example for your team.

### Leveraging Your Influence

Your emotional intelligence empowers you to wield influence effectively. By understanding the emotions and needs of those around you, you can tailor your leadership approach to motivate and inspire. As you build strong relationships based on trust and empathy, your influence as a female leader becomes even more potent, fostering a sense of loyalty and commitment among your team members.

### The Benefits Of Developing Emotional Intelligence

Cultivating emotional intelligence makes you a more compassionate and understanding leader and unlocks your full potential as a trailblazer. By embracing your emotional intelligence, you can:

- foster a culture of inclusion and interpersonal sensitivity
- boost employee engagement,
- improve communication,
- emphasize teamwork and consensus building,
- develop resilience and conflict management skills,
- excel in multitasking
- and drive innovation within your organization.

As you navigate challenges with emotional resilience and empathy, you create a positive and empowering work environment where everyone thrives.

# Developing Your Empathic Edge

Emotional intelligence—is THE empathic edge that sets you apart as a female leader. In this section, you will explore the critical facets of emotional intelligence and learn practical strategies to enhance your EI prowess.

### Understanding Empathy

Lean into the power of empathy—the ability to connect deeply with others' emotions and understand their perspectives. Cultivate active listening skills to truly hear what your team members are saying verbally and non-verbally. Practice putting yourself in their shoes, appreciating their joys and concerns, and offering genuine support. Empathy creates bonds that fuel collaboration, open communication, and a thriving team dynamic.

## 10 Key Factors & Strategies To Enhance Your Empathic Abilities

1. **Use active listening:** Practice active listening by giving your full attention to the speaker. Focus on what they are saying without interrupting or formulating a response in your mind. Pay attention to their tone, body language, and emotions conveyed.

2. **Put yourself in their shoes:** See the situation from the other person's perspective. Imagine what they might be feeling and experiencing at that moment. This exercise helps you gain insight into their emotions and thought processes.

3. **Show genuine interest:** Demonstrate a genuine interest in the person and their feelings. Ask open-ended questions to encourage them to share their thoughts and emotions. Make them feel heard and valued.

4. **Be non-judgmental:** Create a safe and non-judgmental space for the other person to express themselves. Avoid making assumptions or jumping to conclusions about their emotions or experiences.

5. **Observe non-verbal cues:** Pay attention to non-verbal cues like facial expressions, body language, and gestures. These cues can provide valuable insights into the person's emotions, even when they may not explicitly express them verbally.

6. **Practice empathic validation:** Acknowledge and validate the other person's emotions. Show understanding and empathy without trying to fix their problems or dismiss their feelings.

7. **Cultivate emotional awareness:** Develop a firm grasp of your own emotions. When you are more in tune with your own feelings, you can better relate to and understand the emotions of others.

8. **Read empathy-enhancing literature:** Engage with books, movies, or stories that explore diverse perspectives and emotions. This can broaden your understanding of different human experiences and help you empathize more effectively.

9. **Practice empathy daily:** Make a conscious effort to practice empathy in your daily interactions. Whether it's with colleagues, friends, family, or

even strangers, approach each encounter with a compassionate and empathic mindset.

10. **Seek feedback:** Ask for feedback from others about your empathic skills. Seeking feedback allows you to identify areas for improvement and helps you grow as an empathic leader.

# • Emotional Awareness: Navigating The Landscape Of Feelings

Developing emotional awareness starts with understanding your own emotions. Observe your feelings without judgment, acknowledging their presence and impact. By becoming more in tune with your emotional landscape, you can effectively manage your reactions and make informed decisions in the heat of the moment. This self-awareness also enables you to respond thoughtfully to the emotions of others, fostering a culture of empathy and understanding.

## *9 Key Factors & Strategies To Enhance These Crucial Skills*

1. **Mindfulness practice:** Engage in mindfulness activities, such as meditation or deep breathing exercises, to tune into your emotions and thoughts without judgment. Mindfulness helps you become more aware of your emotional responses and triggers.

2. **Journaling:** Maintain a journal to regularly reflect on your emotions, experiences, and reactions. Writing down your thoughts can provide insights into your emotional patterns and help you identify areas for self-improvement.

3. **Use emotion labels:** Practice identifying and labeling your emotions accurately. Use specific words to describe your feelings rather than vague terms. This practice increases emotional clarity and self-awareness.

4. **Practice self-reflection:** Set aside time for self-reflection regularly. Analyze your reactions to different situations to understand the underlying emotions and triggers.

5. **Emotional check-ins:** Take moments throughout the day to check in with your emotions. This brief pause can help you recognize and manage any arising emotions more effectively.

6. **Observe physical responses:** Pay attention to how your body reacts to different emotions. Physical sensations like tension, heart rate, or butterflies in your stomach can indicate underlying emotions.

7. **Embrace vulnerability:** Allow yourself to be vulnerable and open to experiencing various

emotions. Avoid suppressing or denying feelings, as this can hinder self-awareness.

8. **Self-compassion:** Treat yourself with kindness and compassion, especially when dealing with challenging emotions or situations. Be understanding of your own imperfections and learn from them.

9. **Professional development:** Consider attending workshops or training sessions on emotional intelligence and self-awareness. These resources can provide valuable tools and insights.

## • Empowering Influence: Leading With Emotional Intelligence

Leadership is about influence, and emotional intelligence is the key to unlocking your full potential in this domain. Use your empathic skills to understand your team's needs, fears, and aspirations. Tailor your communication to resonate with them, providing encouragement and guidance. Your ability to connect emotionally fosters trust and loyalty, ensuring your influence leaves a lasting, positive impact.

## To Enhance Your Empowering Influence, Consider These 9 Key Strategies

1. **Tailor communication:** Customize your communication style to resonate with each individual on your team. Some team members prefer direct and concise messages, while others appreciate a more personal and detailed approach.

2. **Provide encouragement:** Offer encouragement and praise for a job well done. Acknowledging their efforts boosts morale and motivates them to excel further.

3. **Offer guidance and support:** Be available to advise and support whenever needed. A supportive leader fosters a sense of security and confidence within the team.

4. **Recognize and manage emotions:** Be aware of and manage them effectively, especially in high-stress situations. A composed and emotionally stable leader sets a positive example for the team.

5. **Encourage emotional expression:** Create an environment where team members feel comfortable expressing their emotions and ideas. Encouraging open communication builds trust and psychological safety.

6. **Resolve conflicts with empathy:** When conflicts arise, approach resolution with empathy and a desire to understand each party's perspective. Seek solutions that consider everyone's feelings and needs.

7. **Lead by example:** Model the emotional intelligence you wish to see in your team. Demonstrate self-awareness, empathy, and respectful communication in your interactions.

8. **Promote emotional well-being:** Recognize the importance of emotional well-being in the workplace. Encourage work-life balance, support stress management, and prioritize mental health.

9. **Build strong relationships:** Invest time and effort in building strong relationships with your team members. Positive relationships create a sense of belonging and commitment to shared goals.

## • Resilience: Embracing Challenges With Emotional Fortitude

Resilience is the pillar of emotional intelligence—a quality that helps you weather storms and emerge stronger. Embrace change as an opportunity for growth, and view setbacks as valuable lessons. Tap into your emotional reserves to stay composed during challenging times, inspiring your team to navigate uncertainty gracefully and determinedly. We have covered much about how to develop resilience in chapter 5 but here are some bonus tips for developing resilience.

- **Develop coping strategies:** Identify healthy coping strategies that help you manage stress and build resilience. This could include regular exercise, spending time in nature, journaling, or engaging in creative activities. Find what works best for you and incorporate these practices into your daily routine.

- **Set realistic goals and expectations:** Establish clear and achievable goals for yourself and your team. Setting realistic expectations can prevent feelings of overwhelm and frustration when facing obstacles. Break larger tasks into smaller, manageable steps, celebrating each milestone achieved along the way.

- **Develop problem-solving skills:** Cultivate strong problem-solving skills to approach challenges in a structured and effective manner. Break down complex issues into smaller, manageable parts, and brainstorm potential solutions. Being a proactive problem solver empowers you to take charge and tackle obstacles head-on.

- **Maintain a healthy work-life balance:** Strive for balance between your professional and personal life to avoid burnout and fatigue. Prioritize self-care activities, hobbies, and quality time with loved ones. A well-rested, balanced mind is more resilient and better equipped to handle challenges.

# Case Study — Jacinda Arden's Emotional Intelligence In Action

In the diverse landscape of politics, Jacinda Ardern emerged as a shining example of empathic leadership. As the Prime Minister of New Zealand, she skillfully demonstrated emotional intelligence, interpersonal sensitivity, resilience, and mental toughness, leaving an indelible mark on her nation and the world.

### Emotional Intelligence Amid Tragedy

In March 2019, New Zealand was rocked by a devastating mass shooting in Christchurch, leaving the nation in grief and shock. Jacinda Ardern's response was an embodiment of emotional intelligence. Instead of resorting to anger or fear, she displayed deep empathy for the victims and their families. Jacinda promptly visited the affected communities, comforting them with genuine care and understanding. Her poignant gesture of wearing a headscarf to show solidarity with Muslim women further exemplified her compassionate leadership.

## Navigating The Global Stage

Jacinda's emotional intelligence transcended borders. She deftly navigated diplomatic waters in addressing global issues with her interpersonal sensitivity. Her ability to connect with world leaders personally allowed her to influence meaningful change on pressing matters like climate change and the plight of refugees. Her balanced negotiation approach earned her respect and admiration, strengthening New Zealand's position on the international stage.

## Resilience In The Face Of Adversity

Jacinda's leadership resilience was tested when a catastrophic volcanic eruption struck White Island in 2019. She responded promptly, leading rescue efforts and supporting the victims' families. Her unwavering composure during crises instilled confidence in the nation, inspiring people to unite and rebuild.

## Mental Toughness In The Face Of A Pandemic

During the COVID-19 pandemic, Jacinda Ardern's mental toughness and strength shone through her approach to handling restrictions. While the rest of the world grappled with uncertainty and fluctuating measures, Jacinda made decisive decisions, prioritizing the health and safety of her people. Her empathic communication and transparent leadership during lockdowns reassured the nation, fostering a sense of solidarity and trust in the government's actions.

## Connecting With The Community

Jacinda fostered open communication and genuine connections with her constituents in her day-to-day leadership. She proactively engaged with people from all walks of life, actively listening to their concerns and aspirations. This approach helped her stay attuned to the needs of her nation. It led to implementing policies that addressed real-life challenges faced by her citizens.

## Prioritizing Mental Health And Well-Being

Jacinda recognized the significance of mental health and well-being in her nation's growth and resilience. She focused on initiatives to tackle mental health issues, reduce stigma, and ensure accessible mental health services. Her efforts to prioritize the emotional well-being of her people fostered a culture of compassion and understanding throughout New Zealand.

Through her exemplary leadership, Jacinda Ardern demonstrated that emotional intelligence is an essential quality for leading with brilliance. Her ability to connect with people on an emotional level, navigate complex challenges, and prioritize the well-being of her nation sets her apart as a trailblazer and an empathic role model for leaders worldwide.

120

# Understanding Female Intuition: Unveiling the Mystery

Female intuition, often referred to as women's intuition, is a term used to describe the seemingly innate ability of some women to perceive or understand things without relying on explicit reasoning or evidence. It is a form of intuitive insight that allows women to make decisions, detect subtle cues, and grasp underlying emotions more readily. While the term "female intuition" is not a scientific or technical one, research and anecdotal evidence suggest that women may have a heightened sensitivity to nonverbal cues, emotional expressions, and social dynamics, which can contribute to their perceived intuitive abilities.

## The Science Behind Female Intuition

Scientific studies, such as the one conducted by Dr. Daniel Amen using SPECT (Single Photon Emission Computed Tomography) imaging, revealed fascinating insights into the female brain. It was found that women exhibit more activity in the prefrontal cortex, which governs decision-making and complex thoughts. Additionally, increased blood flow to the limbic area and the hippocampus may contribute to their strengths in decision-making, emotional processing, and memory recall.

In contrast, men tend to have higher blood flow to the visual regions, suggesting that their brains may be more specialized in visual processing tasks. This specialization may be related to spatial navigation, object recognition, and other visual-spatial skills. Men may excel in jobs that require them to quickly process and interpret visual information.

### *The Power Of Intuitive Leadership*

Your intuition serves as an invaluable tool in leadership. Women's ability to read facial expressions and pick up on subtle social cues enables them to connect deeply with others. Embracing and trusting your intuition empowers you to make insightful decisions, anticipate challenges, and build solid and empathetic connections within your team and beyond.

## • Unleash The Hidden Signals

You may sometimes feel like you lack that innate female intuition, but fear not, for it can be nurtured and strengthened with practice. Understanding nonverbal cues, emotional expressions, and social dynamics is within your reach, and it all begins with keen observation and an open mind.

### *Understanding nonverbal cues*

Be keenly aware of body language, gestures, and facial expressions during conversations. Pay attention to subtle shifts in posture, eye contact, and hand movements, as they often reveal unspoken emotions and intentions. Practice mirroring the body language of others to build rapport and make them feel at ease. Over time, you'll become more attuned to these nonverbal cues, enriching your understanding of people's feelings and thoughts.

Mastering the art of understanding nonverbal cues opens a gateway to a world of hidden communication. Body language, gestures, and facial expressions are rich sources of information, offering insights into people's emotions, intentions, and attitudes. To harness this skill, here are some practical tips to help you decode the unspoken language:

- **Eye contact:** Pay attention to the level and duration of eye contact during conversations. Sustained eye contact often signals interest and attentiveness, while avoiding eye contact might indicate discomfort, shyness, or deception.

- **Posture and body positioning:** Observe how individuals hold themselves during different interactions. An open, relaxed posture typically indicates confidence and approachability, while crossed arms or legs might signal defensiveness or discomfort.

- **Smiles:** Different smiles convey various emotions. A genuine smile involves both the mouth and eyes, known as a Duchenne smile. A forced or polite smile, on the other hand, affects only the mouth and lacks warmth.

- **Gestures:** Take note of hand movements and gestures as people speak. Hand movements accompanying speech often emphasize points and clarify another's message. Be mindful of cultural differences, as gestures can carry diverse meanings in different contexts.

- **Mirroring:** Subtly mirror the body language of the person you're conversing with. Mirroring helps build rapport and fosters a sense of connection and understanding.

- **Microexpressions:** Pay attention to fleeting facial expressions, known as microexpressions, which last only for a fraction of a second. These brief expressions often reveal genuine emotions that people might attempt to conceal consciously.

- **Head nods:** Nodding is a nonverbal cue that indicates active listening and agreement. It shows that you are engaged in the conversation and supportive of the speaker's ideas.

- **Proxemics:** Be aware of personal space preferences and how distance affects interactions. Different cultures have varying expectations regarding personal space, so adapt accordingly to respect boundaries.

- **Touch:** Be cautious with touch, as it carries different meanings in different contexts. Some cultures are more comfortable with physical contact, while others prefer more personal space.

- **Regulating speech:** Observe how individuals regulate their speech patterns during conversations. Pausing before speaking might indicate thoughtfulness, while rapid speech might signal excitement or nervousness.

Remember that context is crucial as you immerse yourself in observing and decoding nonverbal cues. Combine your newfound knowledge with active listening and empathy to better understand people's emotions and intentions. By honing this skill, you'll enhance your emotional intelligence, allowing you to connect authentically with others and become a perceptive and influential leader.

## Decoding Emotional Expressions

Take time to read up on various emotions and their associated expressions. Observe people in different situations to identify how they manifest emotions through facial expressions, tone of voice, and gestures. Practice recognizing basic emotions like happiness, sadness, anger, fear, and surprise in others. As you build your emotional vocabulary and awareness, you'll find yourself better equipped to respond empathetically and connect with others on a deeper level.

Here are some ways to improve identifying emotions:

- **Mirror emotions:** Stand before a mirror and practice displaying various emotions. Observe your facial expressions and body language as you replicate feelings like happiness, sadness, surprise, and anger. This exercise helps you understand your own emotional cues.

- **Observe others:** Pay attention to people's facial expressions during everyday interactions. Notice the subtle cues that indicate their emotional state. Practice identifying common emotions like joy, sadness, fear, and excitement in different social settings.

- **Watch emotional movies or shows:** Watch movies or TV shows that evoke strong emotions in characters. Observe their nonverbal cues and try to identify the emotions they are experiencing. This can help you recognize emotional expressions in real-life situations.

- **Read emotional books:** Read books or stories that explore characters' emotions in-depth. Pay attention to the author's descriptions of emotional expressions, and try to visualize how the characters might appear when experiencing different feelings.

- **Practice empathic listening:** When talking to others, focus on listening empathically. Try to sense the emotions behind their words and observe their nonverbal cues. This will help you become more adept at recognizing emotions in real time.

- **Record your observations:** Keep a journal of your observations of emotional expressions you encounter throughout the day. Describe what you noticed and how you interpreted the emotions being conveyed.

- **Group emotion practice:** In group settings, such as meetings or social gatherings, silently observe people's emotional cues. Take note of any patterns or recurring expressions that correspond to specific emotions.

- **Discuss emotions with others:** Engage in open conversations about emotions with friends, family, or colleagues. Sharing perspectives on emotions and nonverbal cues can broaden your understanding and enrich your learning.

Building your ability to recognize basic emotions is gradual, and practice is critical. Be patient with yourself and celebrate your progress along the way. As you become more proficient in identifying emotions, you'll enhance your emotional intelligence, enabling you to connect more deeply with others and easily navigate various social situations.

## Navigating Social Dynamics

Immerse yourself in various social settings and observe the dynamics between individuals or groups. Pay attention to power dynamics, how people assert themselves, and how they respond to different personalities. Observe how social norms and cultural backgrounds influence interactions. Engage in active listening during conversations to understand people's perspectives fully. With time and practice, you'll develop a deeper insight into the intricacies of social dynamics, allowing you to navigate diverse situations more easily.

Remember, developing female intuition is a journey; there's no need to rush. Embrace each interaction as an opportunity to learn and grow. Trust yourself, and give yourself permission to make mistakes. As you continue honing these skills, you'll find that your intuitive leadership becomes more natural and powerful, empowering you to connect authentically, lead with brilliance, and profoundly impact your personal and professional life.

## Some Final Tips For Female Wisdom

- **Breaking Free From Stereotypes**

Society may have perpetuated stereotypes of women as overly emotional or irrational, but science has proven otherwise. Your intuition is not a hindrance; it is your superpower. Embrace it without hesitation or fear of judgment. Trusting your gut feelings can lead you to navigate complex situations with clarity and grace.

- **Taking Charge Of Your Leadership Journey**

Embrace your natural talents and the neural connectors that make your brain more efficient at understanding emotions and social cues. Silence the inner voice that urges you to dismiss your intuition. Instead, empower yourself to lead confidently, relying on logic and intuition. Combining your innate strengths with a growth mindset, emotional intelligence, and resilience will elevate your leadership to unprecedented heights.

- **Reclaim Your Power: Embrace Your Womanhood and Lead Fearlessly**

It's time to reclaim your power and unleash your inherent potential as a woman leader. Embrace your intuition as a formidable asset, navigating the complexities of leadership with clarity and insight. You will rise above challenges, shatter stereotypes, and lead with brilliance by combining your unique qualities, emotional intelligence, and female intuition. Your journey to becoming an extraordinary trailblazer begins by trusting in yourself and embracing all the incredible qualities that set you apart as a woman leader.

## *Up Next?*

After completing this chapter, you should know that as a woman, you possess innate strengths in understanding nonverbal cues, emotional expressions, and social dynamics, which are vital to your intuitive leadership. By embracing your emotional intelligence, you can foster a culture of inclusion, empathy, and collaboration, leading your team with confidence and authenticity. As you continue your journey as a female leader, remember that your intuition is not a hindrance but a formidable asset that sets you apart.

The next chapter will be brimming with practical strategies and real-life examples to revolutionize how you view yourself and your leadership capabilities. Get ready to tap into your inner power, embrace your authentic self, and cultivate unshakeable confidence.

# Chapter 7: Unleash Your Inner Confidence: Strategies For Immediate Transformation

In your professional and personal life, confidence forms the bedrock of success. Challenges are inevitable as you embark on your journey to reach your full potential, but remember this: you are strong, capable, and equipped to conquer them all. Your mission is to push forward, strive, and thrive. Building unwavering confidence and understanding your intrinsic worth will be the key to overcoming obstacles and achieving your most audacious goals.

Now, the time has come to unlock the empowering potential of self-assurance through practical strategies you can implement immediately. This chapter will delve into the potent effectiveness of the Emotional Freedom Technique (EFT), the art of visualization, and the mastery of confident body language. Each tool will become a pillar of your newfound confidence, ready to elevate you to new heights of self-belief.

Before we plunge into the highly enabling techniques that await you, keep these 10 empowering tips at the forefront of your mind. Embrace them to strengthen your journey towards greater self-confidence and the authentic expression of your unique self:

- **Set achievable goals:** Avoid overwhelm by breaking your ambitions into manageable steps.

- **Speak your truth:** Let your voice be heard with conviction, as your opinions are valuable.

- **Tame your inner critic:** Cultivate self-compassion and silence the voice of self-doubt.

- **Embrace failure:** Embrace setbacks as stepping stones to growth and resilience.

- **Reinforce your strengths:** Celebrate your capabilities with positive affirmations.

- **Radiate confidence:** Hold your head high, embodying the belief that you are capable.

- **Command with body language:** Master the art of confident body language to exude assurance.

- **Embrace risks:** Step out of your comfort zone and embark on a growth journey.

- **Embody positivity:** Choose uplifting words that nurture your self-belief and inspire others.

- **Harness the power of visualization:** Unlock your full potential through the art of vivid imagination.

With these empowering tactics in your arsenal, you can take another leap forward on your self-assured journey, becoming the influential, poised, and unshakable leader you are destined to be. Let us venture together and unleash the effective, authentic leader within you!

# Tap Into The Emotional Freedom Technique To Change Your Inner

# Critic

As a realistic and grounded woman, you know that everyone deals with that annoying inner critic—the one that seems to narrate your life in the most obnoxious ways possible. This voice isn't kind and can make you question yourself, leaving you feeling inadequate and impacting your self-esteem. But fear not, for you have the power to overcome it with the highly effective Emotional Freedom Technique (EFT).

## *Emotional Freedom Technique (EFT)*

Also known as "tapping," EFT is a therapeutic technique that combines elements of traditional Chinese medicine, cognitive psychology, and exposure therapy. While more research is still needed to fully understand its mechanisms, there are several proposed reasons why EFT may work:

1. **Stress reduction:** Tapping on specific acupressure points is believed to activate the body's relaxation response, reducing the production of stress hormones like cortisol. This can help calm the nervous system and alleviate anxiety and stress.

2. **Disruption of neural pathways:** Tapping on acupressure points while focusing on a negative emotion or thought is believed to interrupt the brain's emotional processing pathways. This

disruption can lead to a decrease in the emotional intensity associated with the specific thought or memory.

3. **Normalization of energy flow:** In traditional Chinese medicine, it is believed that energy, or "qi," flows through meridians in the body. Negative emotions and experiences can disrupt this energy flow. EFT aims to restore energy balance and promote emotional well-being by tapping on specific points.

4. **Combination of cognitive and exposure techniques:** EFT combines verbalizing specific thoughts or emotions with physical tapping. This dual-action approach may help individuals confront and process distressing emotions more effectively.

5. **Association and desensitization:** The tapping process involves associating negative emotions with specific physical sensations (tapping) and gradually desensitizing the individual to those emotions. Over time, this can lead to a reduction in the emotional charge associated with the particular issue.

6. **Self-acceptance and self-compassion:** Positive affirmations during EFT can foster self-acceptance and self-compassion. Individuals can cultivate a more positive self-perception by focusing on self-empowering statements while tapping.

**How To Use It**

### Identify The Inner Critic

Take a moment to recognize when your inner critic surfaces. What are the specific negative thoughts it throws your way? Write them down, bringing them into the light.

### Tapping Technique

EFT involves tapping on specific acupressure points while acknowledging the negative thoughts. This helps to release their emotional hold on you. To begin, gently tap with your fingertips on the following points using two to three fingers:

- Top of the head
- Eyebrow
- Side of the eye
- Under the eye
- Under the nose
- Chin
- Collarbone
- Under the arm
- Wrists (tap them together)

### Affirmations & Reframing

As you tap on each point, acknowledge and voice the negative thought, then follow it with a positive affirmation or reframing. For example:

- *Tap on the eyebrow point:* "Even though my inner critic says I'm not good enough, I deeply and completely love and accept myself."
- *Tap under the eye:* "I release this self-doubt and embrace my worth and capabilities."
- *Repeat the process for each acupressure point,* customizing the affirmations to address your specific negative thoughts.
- Breathe & Release

Take deep breaths as you tap and allow yourself to release the negative emotions tied to the inner critic's words. Feel the emotional weight lifting off your shoulders.

## *Using EFT In Real-Life Situations*

Conquering Pre-Interview Nerves
Before an interview, tap on acupressure points and affirm:

- *Top of the head:* "I am well-prepared and confident."
- *Eyebrow:* "I trust in my skills and qualifications."
- *Side of the eye:* "I make a positive and lasting impression."
- *Under the eye:* "I release self-doubt and embrace my potential."
- *Under the nose:* "I am worthy of this opportunity."
- *Chin:* "I am authentic, and I trust myself."

- *Collarbone:* "I am ready to showcase my abilities."
- *Under the arm:* "I let go of past interview experiences."
- *Wrists (tap together):* "I am confident and prepared."

## Overcoming Procrastination & Taking Action

To beat procrastination, tap on acupressure points and affirm:

- *Top of the head:* "I can take action."
- *Eyebrow:* "I release resistance and choose progress."
- *Side of the eye:* "I am capable and can overcome doubts."
- *Under the eye:* "I embrace growth and learn from experiences."
- *Under the nose:* "I focus on productive tasks, no distractions."
- *Chin:* "I am committed to success; I believe in myself."
- *Collarbone:* "I prioritize and take control of my time."
- *Under the arm:* "I let go of perfectionism, one step at a time."
- *Wrists (tap together):* "I am proactive, determined, and achieving."

### Before A Big Presentation

If your inner critic fills you with self-doubt before an important presentation, take a moment in the restroom or private space. Tap on the acupressure points, affirming, "I am well-prepared and confident in my abilities. I have valuable insights to share with the audience."

### Overcoming Social Anxiety

When attending a social event where your inner critic tells you you'll be awkward and out of place, find a quiet spot, tap, and affirm, "I am worthy of connection, and I can engage with others authentically and confidently."

Remember, EFT is a powerful tool you can use anytime and anywhere to shift your perspective and nurture self-compassion. By tapping into this empowering technique, you can reclaim your inner power and silence the inner critic, paving the way for unshakeable self-confidence in your personal and professional life.

# The Power Of Visualization For Increased Confidence

Visualization is a potent tool that can propel you toward success and fulfillment in your professional and personal life. But what exactly is visualization? It's the act of vividly picturing something in your mind, whether it's your desired achievements, a serene lakeside view for relaxation, or any vision that brings you joy. It's a way to momentarily escape from the hustle and bustle, granting your mind the much-needed respite to shed stress and re-energize.

Why should you embrace visualization? When you visualize your goals and aspirations, you build confidence and ignite the motivation to pursue them. By mentally envisioning yourself succeeding, you reinforce the belief that you are capable of achieving greatness.

The science behind visualization lies in its ability to create neural patterns similar to those formed during real-life experiences. Your brain responds to visualization as if you were actively engaged in the made-up scenario. This stimulates your nervous system, driving you to take actions that align with your visualized goals.

## *How To Use Visualization*

Let's walk through a practical example to guide you through the steps of visualization:

1. **Find a quiet space:** Sit comfortably in a quiet room, free from distractions. Take a moment to settle in and relax your body.

2. **Relaxation breathing:** Close your eyes and take several deep breaths. Inhale slowly and deeply,

then exhale fully. Feel the tension leaving your body with each breath.

3. **Clarify your vision:** Imagine yourself in a scenario where you need confidence and assertiveness. Perhaps something like giving a presentation at work. Picture yourself speaking with clarity and enthusiasm, engaging your audience effortlessly. Visualize them nodding in agreement and being inspired by your words.

4. **Embrace the emotions:** As you continue to visualize, tap into the positive emotions that come with success. Feel the thrill of accomplishment, the satisfaction of connecting with others, and the pride of a well-done job.

5. **Stay present:** Keep your focus on the present moment of visualization. Don't worry about past failures or future doubts. Just immerse yourself in the empowering experience you've created.

6. **Consistency matters:** Dedicate just five to ten minutes daily to visualization. Regular practice strengthens your motivation and focus.

Visualization empowers you to overcome obstacles, regain focus, and boost productivity. As a confident, assertive woman, you can use visualization to prepare for important presentations, master the art of public speaking, inspire your team with innovative ideas, or even conquer personal goals or skills like skating, riding a bike, or driving.

# Case Study — Serena Williams: A Champion's Vision

Let's delve into the inspiring journey of Serena Williams, a renowned tennis champion who has harnessed the power of visualization to achieve remarkable success in her athletic career.

From a young age, Serena Williams had a burning desire to become one of the greatest tennis players in history. As a child, she and her sister Venus would often visualize themselves winning prestigious tennis tournaments while practicing on public courts in Compton, California. Serena vividly imagined herself standing on the grand stages of Wimbledon, the US Open, and the French Open, holding trophies high above her head as the crowd cheered her name.

Serena faced numerous challenges through her journey to the top, including injuries, setbacks, and fierce competitors. However, she remained steadfast in her commitment to visualizing her path to greatness. Before each match, Serena would close her eyes and imagine the perfect execution of her serves, groundstrokes, and volleys. She would see herself moving swiftly across the court, anticipating her opponents' shots with uncanny precision and celebrating her well-deserved victories with unbridled joy.

Serena's visualizations went beyond match scenarios. She envisioned herself enduring rigorous training sessions, pushing her body to its limits, and overcoming physical and mental hurdles. Her visualizations encompassed on-court excellence and the mental fortitude required to maintain her focus and composure during challenging moments.

As Serena's tennis career soared, she faced immense pressure to maintain her dominance. She channeled the power of visualization to stay centered amid the expectations and scrutiny. Before significant tournaments, she would mentally rehearse her match strategies and remind herself of her countless accomplishments, building the confidence necessary to perform at her peak.

The culmination of Serena Williams' unwavering belief in the power of visualization came at the 2017 Australian Open. During her pregnancy, Serena continued to visualize herself triumphantly returning to competitive tennis. She saw herself defying the odds, reclaiming her place at the top, and proving that motherhood and athletic success could coexist. Serena secured her 23rd Grand Slam title in a thrilling final, setting a new record for the Open Era.

Beyond her athletic achievements, Serena's visualizations extended to other aspects of her life. She visualized herself as a role model, empowering young girls worldwide to pursue their dreams with courage and resilience. Serena envisioned herself using her platform to advocate for women's rights, equal pay, and social justice causes.

Serena Williams' journey exemplifies the revolutionary power of visualization. Through mentally rehearsing her success, Serena conquered the tennis world and became an iconic symbol of excellence, strength, and determination. Her story serves as a testament to the unlimited potential that lies within each of us when we dare to envision greatness and relentlessly pursue our dreams.

By following Serena's lead and adopting visualization as a powerful tool, you can unlock the doors to your dreams, build unshakable confidence, and create a path to success that aligns with your deepest aspirations. As you close your eyes and visualize your journey, remember that the seeds of greatness lie within you, waiting to bloom through the power of visualization.

# Body Language For Confidence: Exuding Power & Presence

As a woman seeking to cultivate unshakable confidence, mastering the art of body language can be a game-changer in how you are perceived and respected. Building confidence is not an overnight process, especially if you are naturally introverted or face gender-related challenges. However, understanding and utilizing your body language can give you a significant advantage in commanding attention and influencing others positively.

### The Impact Of Confident Body Language

Your body language serves as a powerful form of non-verbal communication. It is one of the first things people notice when interacting with you. When you project confidence through your body language, others are more likely to take you seriously, listen to your ideas, and acknowledge your worth. On the other hand, if your body language reflects insecurity or nervousness, it may hinder your ability to convey your message effectively.

### Mastering Confident Body Language: Key Tips

- **Maintain empowering eye contact:** Make an effort to hold eye contact when speaking with others. Steady eye contact portrays confidence, engagement, and sincerity. However, avoid excessive staring, as it may feel intimidating. Strike a balance that reflects your assertiveness and warmth.

- **Lean forward to show interest:** When listening to others, lean slightly forward to show that you are engaged and genuinely interested in the conversation. This body language demonstrates active listening and establishes a connection with the speaker.

- **Posture–stand tall and proud:** Your posture speaks volumes about your confidence. Stand up straight with your shoulders back, signaling poise and self-assuredness. Avoid slouching, as it may convey insecurity.

- **Be mindful of fidgeting:** Be aware of fidgeting tendencies, such as playing with your hair or putting your hands in your pockets. Minimize these gestures, as they can be perceived as signs of nervousness or anxiety.

- **Control your pace:** Speak deliberately and avoid rushing through your words. Speaking too quickly may signal nervousness or a lack of conviction. Take the time to articulate your thoughts clearly and with purpose.

- **Use assertive handshakes:** When shaking hands, offer a firm and confident grip. This handshake conveys self-assurance and leaves a lasting positive impression.

- **Mirror the body language of others:** Subtly mirror the body language of those you interact with, especially if they display confident postures. Mirroring fosters rapport and shows attentiveness to the conversation.

- **Act "As If"–Harness the power of mindset:** Embody the confidence you aspire to by adopting the "act as if" mindset. Even if you don't feel entirely confident in a particular situation, behaving as if you are confident can influence how others perceive you and, more importantly, how you perceive yourself. The "act as if" approach can help rewire your brain and reinforce positive self-beliefs, gradually boosting your genuine confidence.

By incorporating these essential tips and embracing the "act as if" mindset, you can transform your body language to reflect the inner strength and self-assurance that lies within you. Over time, practicing confident body language will become second nature, empowering you to navigate life and leadership with unshakeable poise and presence.

## Overcoming Body Issues: Projecting

Addressing and overcoming body issues that are common among women can further enhance your confident body language. Embracing your authentic self and dispelling societal beauty standards will empower you to project power and presence.

- **Challenge unrealistic beauty ideals:** Disregard narrow beauty standards and embrace your unique form. Celebrate your individuality and recognize that true beauty comes from authenticity.

- **Practice self-compassion:** Be kind to yourself and focus on your strengths and capabilities. Cultivating self-compassion will combat negative self-perceptions and reinforce your self-assurance.

- **Focus on what your body can do:** Shift your focus from appearance to functionality. Engage in activities that make you feel strong and capable, reinforcing a positive self-image.

- **Surround yourself with positive influences:** Surround yourself with supportive individuals who appreciate and celebrate you for who you are. Positive influences build confidence and empower you to project your presence with authenticity.

# Case Study — Malala Yousafzai: Empowering Presence Through Confident Body Language

Get ready to be inspired by the incredible journey of Malala Yousafzai, the renowned Pakistani activist and Nobel Laureate, whose story is a testament to the empowering power of confident body language. Malala's remarkable journey began in the Swat Valley of Pakistan, where she fearlessly advocated for girls' education despite the dangers posed by the Taliban's oppressive regime.

In 2012, at just 15 years old, Malala survived an assassination attempt by the Taliban, who sought to silence her advocacy. Miraculously recovering from the attack, she refused to back down and continued her mission with unwavering determination. In the face of adversity, Malala's resilience and courage captured the world's attention, turning her into a symbol of hope and empowerment for girls and women everywhere.

What sets Malala apart as a role model for empowering presence through confident body language is her ability to communicate with conviction and authenticity. Despite facing life-threatening challenges, Malala never allowed fear to dictate her actions. Instead, she stood tall and resolute, maintaining firm eye contact that beamed with unwavering resolve. Her pace and tone of voice were steady and purposeful, carrying the weight of her steadfast commitment to her cause.

Malala's commanding presence extends beyond the podium. Even during her meetings with world leaders and influential figures, she exudes an air of authority and self-assurance. Her compelling body language is evident as she leans forward to show genuine interest when listening to others, making them feel heard and valued.

Every movement is purposeful and impactful when she gestures, reinforcing her messages with genuine emotion. Her expressive hand movements enhance the power of her words, reflecting her passion and dedication to her advocacy. It's not just about what Malala says or does; it's about the impact she creates through her clear body language.

Her posture exudes confidence and poise, reflecting her unshakable commitment to her cause. Standing tall and proud, Malala projects an image of strength that commands respect from everyone she encounters. Her confident body language communicates that she is unyielding in her beliefs and committed to fighting for positive change.

Beyond her words, Malala's powerful presence is also reflected in her choice of dress. Embracing her cultural identity, she wears traditional Pakistani attire with pride, showing the world that embracing one's roots and heritage is a source of strength.

Malala's assertive body language has resonated with millions of girls and women worldwide, inspiring them to embrace their voices and fight for change in their communities. Through her confident presence, Malala has sparked a global movement that designates young women as agents of change, shattering barriers and transforming lives.

As we explore Malala's journey, we can draw valuable lessons on cultivating our emphatic presence through confident body language. Embracing the essence of authentic leadership, we can learn to stand tall, make our voices heard, and unapologetically pursue our passions.

Malala Yousafzai serves as a guiding light, showing us that confidence isn't just a superficial attribute; it's the core of our ability to create change. By looking to her as a role model, we can learn to channel our inner strength, even in the face of adversity. Embracing her fearless spirit, we can authorize ourselves and others to shatter barriers and make a lasting impact on the world. Let Malala's remarkable journey be the inspiration that propels us forward. Embrace the tremendous power of confident body language and let it amplify our voices.

### Up Next?

In this chapter, you were introduced to powerful strategies for immediate transformation. You learned about Emotional Freedom Technique (EFT), or tapping to silence your inner critic and restore emotional well-being. Visualization was emphasized to boost confidence and align your brain with success. Additionally, you explored the significance of confident body language to project assertiveness. Hopefully, you were also inspired by the stories of some of the world's most confident women and how they became this way.

Armed with these tools, you're now ready to embrace your journey toward greater self-confidence and self-expression. Next, in Chapter 8, we'll delve into building courage—a powerful ally in your pursuit of unshakable confidence and assertiveness.

# Chapter 8: Embracing Courage: Unlocking Unshakable Confidence

*"Courage starts with showing up and letting ourselves be seen."*

*— Brené Brown, researcher, author, and public speaker championing vulnerability and resilience.*

Welcome to Chapter 8, where we embark on a journey to unlock the metamorphic power of courage—a force that will empower you to become a more confident woman. In the words of the esteemed writer and diarist Anais Nin,

*"Life shrinks or expands in proportion to one's courage."*

This profound quote reminds us that embracing courage is not merely an option but the essence of growth and self-discovery.

Anais Nin, an avant-garde author known for exploring human emotions and the complexities of relationships, understood the profound impact of courage on one's life. Through her writings, she inspired generations to step beyond the confines of fear and embrace the unknown with audacity and grace. Her quote resonates deeply with our pursuit of confidence and assertiveness, reminding us that the choices we make in moments of courage hold power to shape the very fabric of our existence.

As we venture into the realm of courage, we will witness its profound influence on our brain pathways. The brain is a marvel of adaptability, constantly rewiring itself based on our experiences and actions. By daring to embrace courage in our personal and professional lives, we set in motion a process of neuroplasticity. This rewiring enhances our ability to cultivate unshakable confidence.

Let us dare to embrace courage with open arms. As we venture deeper into the chapters ahead, we will uncover strategies to cultivate courage in our daily lives. Together, we will tap into the wellspring of inner strength that lies within us, and with each courageous step we take, we will expand the boundaries of our lives and emerge as the confident, assertive women we are destined to be.

# The Courage—Confidence Connection

*"When I dare to be powerful, to use my strength in the service of my vision, then it becomes less and less important whether I am afraid."*

– Audre Lorde, writer, feminist, and civil rights activist.

In our quest to become more confident and assertive, we must first understand the profound and beneficial relationship between courage and confidence. As we delve into the neuroscience of courage and its impact on our brain pathways, we will unlock the key to cultivating unshakable self-assurance. By exploring how embracing courage reshapes our thoughts and emotions, we empower ourselves to overcome self-doubt and step into the realm of unwavering confidence.

## The Neuroscience Of Courage & Confidence

Deep within the intricate pathways of our brains lies the foundation of our emotions and behaviors. The amygdala, an almond-shaped structure nestled in the limbic system, plays a pivotal role in processing emotions, including fear and anxiety. When faced with challenges, the amygdala activates the "fight or flight" response, triggering a cascade of physiological changes to protect us from potential threats.

Yet, within this biology of fear lies a remarkable opportunity for growth and transformation. The key to unlocking our potential and kicking fear's butt to the curb lies in the brain's reward system, where dopamine, a neurotransmitter associated with pleasure and motivation, comes into play. When we dare to embrace courage and face our fears, the brain releases dopamine, rewarding and reinforcing the courageous behavior and making us more likely to repeat it.

Repeated acts of courage lead to a fascinating phenomenon known as fear extinction, where the brain's fear response is gradually reduced. This process occurs through a mechanism called "extinction learning," where new, positive associations replace old fear-based ones. Over time, the amygdala becomes less reactive to previously anxiety-inducing stimuli, empowering us to approach challenges more easily and confidently.

As we navigate life with courage, we also cultivate resilience—a powerful psychological resource that bolsters our self-efficacy. When we encounter setbacks or failures and choose to persevere, we build a profound belief in our ability to overcome obstacles. This self-efficacy, in turn, becomes the bedrock of our confidence.

## The Bold Brain: Rewiring For Confidence

The brain is a marvel of adaptability, capable of forming new connections and rewiring itself based on our experiences and actions. This neuroplasticity is a hallmark of our brain's ability to learn, grow, and change throughout our lives. By embracing courage, you can set in motion a process of rewiring your brain to support your journey toward greater confidence.

The prefrontal cortex, the brain's executive center, plays a critical role in decision-making, problem-solving, and regulating emotions. As you engage in courageous acts, the prefrontal cortex comes into play, helping you weigh risks and rewards more effectively. By consciously choosing courage over fear, you will strengthen these neural connections, enhancing your ability to make bold decisions with clarity and conviction.

Furthermore, the prefrontal cortex's involvement in emotional regulation contributes to your sense of self-control and emotional resilience. As you face fears head-on and manage your emotional responses, you gain mastery over your emotions, reducing their influence on your self-confidence.

Similarly, the brain's mirror neuron system comes into play when we witness others' courageous actions. These neurons fire when we perform an action and when we observe someone else doing the same. When we see acts of courage in others, our mirror neurons create empathetic connections, inspiring us to take courageous steps ourselves.

## Courage & Confidence: A Virtuous Cycle

Another benefit of the relationship between courage and confidence is that it forms a virtuous cycle, each feeding and reinforcing the other. As you muster the courage to step out of your comfort zones, confront fears, and embrace challenges, you experience the rush of dopamine and the satisfaction of facing adversity head-on.

This surge of positive emotions translates into heightened self-assurance, validating your belief in your capabilities. With every courageous act, your confidence grows, leading you to take even bolder steps in the future. The virtuous cycle continues as courage fuels confidence, and confidence, in turn, empowers us to be even more courageous.

In this cycle of growth and change, you will move from strength to strength, leaving behind the shackles of self-doubt and hesitation. Your willingness to embrace courage catalyzes a profound internal shift, shaping you into the confident and assertive woman you should aspire to be.

In the upcoming sections, you will explore strategies to cultivate courage daily, empowering you to surmount obstacles and embrace the bold, confident woman you will become.

# Strategies For Embracing Courage

In this section, you'll delve into practical strategies for embracing courage personally and professionally. Courage is not the absence of fear but rather the willingness to act despite it.

> *"You get in life what you have the courage to ask for."*
>
> *- Oprah Winfrey*

Daring to take courageous steps will pave the way for increased confidence, unlocking your true potential. Let's explore various empowering strategies that will help you cultivate courage and unleash your inner strength.

## • Embrace Vulnerability As A Strength

Often, we associate vulnerability with weakness, but in reality, it is a powerful catalyst for courage and growth. Embracing vulnerability means acknowledging your emotions and being open about your fears and uncertainties. By allowing yourself to be vulnerable, you create authentic connections with others and foster a supportive environment. Courageously sharing your thoughts and feelings with trusted individuals can provide invaluable insights and encouragement, ultimately boosting your self-confidence.

Research has shown that embracing vulnerability can increase resilience and emotional well-being. Brené Brown, a renowned researcher, and author, discovered that vulnerability is the birthplace of courage, creativity, and innovation. Daring to be vulnerable opens the door to deeper self-awareness and a richer, more fulfilling life.

Here are a few tips to help you cultivate vulnerability as a source of empowerment:

- **Practice self-reflection:** Identify areas where you may be avoiding vulnerability. Reflect on past experiences and consider how embracing vulnerability could have led to deeper connections or personal growth.

- **Share your story:** Open up and share your experiences, challenges, and triumphs with trusted friends or family members. Showing vulnerability allows others to see your authentic self, including your fears and insecurities. Sharing your story can lead to stronger bonds and a sense of community.

- **Express your emotions:** Allow yourself to feel and express a wide range of emotions. Avoid suppressing feelings of sadness, fear, or uncertainty. When you acknowledge and express your emotions, you create space for healing and personal growth.

- **Set boundaries:** Embracing vulnerability doesn't mean sharing every aspect of your life with everyone. Set healthy boundaries and choose when and with whom you share your thoughts and feelings. Trust is essential in vulnerability, so share it with those who have earned it.

- **Challenge perfectionism:** Let go of the belief that you must be perfect or have all the answers. Vulnerability embraces imperfections and acknowledges that growth comes from learning and accepting ourselves as we are.

- **Embrace uncertainty:** Embracing vulnerability often involves stepping into the unknown. Embrace uncertainty as an opportunity for growth and exploration. Welcome the idea that taking risks and being vulnerable can lead to new experiences and opportunities.

## • Challenge Limiting Beliefs

We all carry limiting beliefs—those deeply ingrained thoughts that keep us from pursuing our dreams. These beliefs are often rooted in past experiences, societal expectations, or self-doubt. To embrace courage fully, we must challenge these limiting beliefs and rewrite the narratives that no longer serve us.

Start by identifying your limiting beliefs. Reflect on times when you hesitated due to self-doubt or fear of failure. Question the validity of these beliefs and seek evidence to challenge them. Replace limiting thoughts with affirmations that empower you. For instance, transform "I'm not good enough" into "I am capable and deserving of success."

Over time, as you confront and dismantle these limiting beliefs, you will develop a newfound sense of courage and self-belief, paving the way for increased confidence and assertiveness.

Here are a few short tips to help you overcome those limiting beliefs:

- **Question your beliefs:** Take a closer look at the ideas that hold you back. Ask yourself if they are based on facts or if they are assumptions you've accepted over time. Challenge the validity of these beliefs.

- **Collect evidence:** Look for evidence that contradicts your limiting beliefs. Seek examples of women who have defied similar beliefs and achieved success. This can help you see that your beliefs are not universal truths.

- **Set realistic goals:** Break down your larger goals into smaller, achievable steps. Setting and reaching realistic milestones can boost your confidence and help you challenge the belief that you can't succeed.

- **Embrace failure as a learning opportunity:** See failure as a natural part of growth and learning. When you encounter setbacks, view them as opportunities to learn and improve rather than evidence of your limitations.

- **Challenge the status quo:**

> *"Taking risks and challenging the status quo are essential if we want to achieve more and reach our full potential." - Sheryl Sandberg.*

Don't be afraid to challenge societal norms or traditional gender roles perpetuating limiting beliefs. Embrace your unique strengths and capabilities, regardless of societal expectations.

# • Step Out Of Your Comfort Zone

Courage thrives in the realm of discomfort. To expand your courage and confidence, make it a habit to step out of your comfort zone regularly. Start with small, manageable challenges and gradually push yourself to take on more significant risks.

Whether it's speaking up in a meeting, trying a new skill, or networking with strangers, each step outside your comfort zone will fortify your courage muscle. Embrace the mindset that failure is an opportunity for growth and learning. Remember that regardless of the outcome, each attempt brings you closer to becoming a more confident and assertive woman.

Try the following tips for ways you can begin to step outside your comfort zone immediately:

- **Strike up a conversation with a stranger:** Challenge yourself to initiate a conversation with someone you don't know, whether it's a colleague at work, a fellow commuter, or someone waiting in line at a coffee shop. Start with a simple compliment or a friendly greeting, and let the conversation flow naturally. Engaging with new people can boost your social skills and expand your network, leading to new opportunities and connections.

- **Try a new hobby or activity:** Take up a hobby or activity you've always wanted to try but felt hesitant about. It could be dancing, painting, a fitness class, or even joining a book club. Stepping into unfamiliar territory can be intimidating but opens the door to learning and personal growth. Embrace the learning process, and don't be afraid to make mistakes.

- **Embrace spontaneity:** Break free from rigid routines occasionally and embrace spontaneity. Say "yes" to impromptu plans or invitations, and be open to unexpected experiences. Embracing spontaneity fosters adaptability and a sense of adventure, making you more confident in navigating uncertain situations.

- **Take solo adventures:** Venture out to places you've never been on your own, such as a museum, park, or nearby town. Exploring independently allows you to rely on your instincts and decision-making skills, boosting your self-reliance and adaptability. Enjoy the freedom of experiencing new things at your own pace.

Remember, stepping out of your comfort zone doesn't always have to involve grand gestures. It's about embracing the small opportunities for growth and challenging yourself in various aspects of life. You'll find that your comfort zone expands by gradually pushing your boundaries. In proportion to it, so will your confidence and assertiveness.

*"Life begins at the end of your comfort zone."*

*- Neale Donald Walsch, spiritual author and thought leader*

## • Cultivate A Growth Mindset

As discussed in chapter 5, a growth mindset is the belief that our abilities and intelligence can be developed through dedication and hard work. Embracing a growth mindset empowers you to see challenges as opportunities and setbacks as stepping stones to success.

When you encounter difficulties, approach them with curiosity and resilience. Embrace the process of learning and improvement. You will navigate challenges with courage and determination by viewing them as chances to grow, elevating your self-assurance and adaptability. Look back to the tips contained within chapter 5 if you need some prompts to remember some ways to cultivate a growth and positive mindset.

## • Seek Support & Inspiration

Courage thrives in the company of supportive individuals. Surround yourself with people who uplift and inspire you. Seek mentors, role models, and like-minded individuals who have embraced courage.

Engage in conversations and share experiences with those encouraging you to take bold steps. Their support and encouragement will provide you with the confidence to face challenges head-on and become a more assertive and empowered woman.

Here are three suggestions for ways you can find the encouragement you need:

- **Join empowering communities:** Seek out groups, clubs, or online communities focused on personal growth, empowerment, and self-development. These spaces provide a supportive network of like-minded individuals who share similar aspirations. Engaging with others who are on similar journeys can inspire you, offer valuable insights, and create a sense of camaraderie. Being part of such a community can be immensely motivating, whether it's a women's leadership group, a confidence-building workshop, or an online forum.

- **Mentorship and role models:** Look for those who embody the qualities you aspire to develop. Mentors can provide guidance, share their experiences, and offer constructive feedback. Learning from someone who has overcome challenges and achieved success can empower and inspire you to persevere. If you can't find a physical mentor, consider reading biographies or watching interviews of inspiring women who have made a difference in their fields.

- **Personal growth books and podcasts:** Immerse yourself in books and podcasts that focus on personal growth, self-confidence, and courage. There are plenty of resources available that offer practical tips, insightful stories, and motivational content. Whether books on building resilience, podcasts on assertive communication, or TED Talks on courage, these resources can provide constant inspiration and knowledge.

## • Practice Mindfulness & Self-Compassion

Mindfulness and self-compassion are essential tools in cultivating courage. Mindfulness involves being present in the moment, acknowledging your thoughts and emotions without judgment. By practicing mindfulness, you can observe your fears and anxieties without becoming overwhelmed by them.

Combine mindfulness with self-compassion—a gentle and understanding attitude toward yourself. Treat yourself with the kindness and compassion you would offer a friend facing challenges. By nurturing self-compassion, you create a safe space to explore and embrace courage, fostering an environment for growth and self-discovery.

Research has shown that mindfulness and self-compassion can positively impact the brain, promoting emotional regulation and reducing stress. As you build these practices into your daily life, you will develop the resilience and emotional balance needed to embrace courage fully.

Here are a couple of quick suggestions for practicing mindfulness and self-compassion in your everyday routine:

• **Nature connection:** Spend time in nature to foster mindfulness and self-compassion. Take a leisurely walk in the park, sit by a serene lake, or hike through the woods. As you immerse yourself in nature, pay attention to your surroundings with all your senses. Feel the gentle breeze on your skin, listen to the soothing sounds of birdsong or rustling leaves, and notice the vibrant colors and textures around you. Mindfully connecting with nature lets you be present in the moment, providing peace and grounding. Embrace the beauty of the natural world and extend that same appreciation and compassion to yourself.

- **Mindful eating:** Transform your eating habits into a mindful practice of self-compassion. Before each meal, take a moment to express gratitude for the nourishment you are about to receive. As you eat, savor each bite slowly and attentively. Notice the flavors, textures, and sensations as you chew. Avoid distractions such as screens or rushing through meals. By eating mindfully, you become more attuned to your body's hunger and fullness cues, fostering a compassionate relationship with yourself and your body's needs.

# • Set Courageous Goals

Setting courageous goals involves dreaming big and daring to pursue audacious aspirations. Break free from the confines of mediocrity and set goals that inspire and challenge you. As you design your path towards these objectives, envision yourself taking courageous steps to achieve them.

Write down your goals and create an action plan with specific milestones. Each step towards your goal will require courage and determination. Celebrate your progress along the way, as each achievement builds your confidence and reinforces your ability to overcome obstacles.

Try out these suggestions for ways to set courageous goals:

- **Dream big and identify your passions:** Allow yourself to dream big and identify the goals that ignite your passions. Reflect on what excites and motivates you, even if it feels daring or unconventional. Setting courageous goals starts with embracing and daring to pursue your aspirations with conviction.

- **Break goals into smaller steps:** Turning courageous dreams into reality may seem daunting initially, but breaking them down into smaller, achievable steps can make the journey more manageable and less overwhelming. Here's how to do it:

    1. *Define the ultimate goal:* Start by clarifying your ultimate courageous goal. What do you want to achieve, and why is it important? Understanding the significance of the goal will provide you with the drive and

determination needed to overcome obstacles.

2. *Identify milestones:* Once you have your ultimate goal, identify critical milestones or checkpoints. These are significant achievements that signify progress toward your goal. Milestones help you track your advancement, maintain focus, and celebrate the journey.

3. *Set specific and measurable objectives:* With milestones in mind, break your courageous goal into specific and measurable objectives. Each objective should be clear, achievable, and time-bound. This approach enables you to monitor your progress and make adjustments as needed.

4. *Plan and prioritize:* Develop a well-structured plan that outlines the steps required to reach each objective. Prioritize the tasks based on their importance and impact on your overall goal. Having a plan in place will provide you with a roadmap for success.

5. *Celebrate achievements:* As you conquer each smaller goal or milestone, celebrate your achievements. Acknowledge the effort you've put in and the progress you've made. Celebrating milestones reinforces your

sense of accomplishment and motivates you to keep moving forward.

6. *Embrace flexibility:* While having a plan is essential, remaining flexible and adaptable is equally important. Life is unpredictable, and challenges may arise unexpectedly. Embrace change when necessary, and view detours as opportunities for growth and learning.

7. *Seek support and accountability:* Enlist the help of friends, family, or mentors who believe in your courageous goals. Sharing your aspirations with others can provide encouragement, guidance, and a sense of accountability. Knowing that others are cheering you on can boost your confidence and determination.

8. *Embrace failure as a stepping stone:* Understand that setbacks and failures are a natural part of any journey. Instead of seeing them as roadblocks, view them as valuable learning experiences. Embracing failure as a stepping stone to success will bolster your resilience and fortify your determination to persevere.

# Case Study —Amelia Earhart:

# Soaring Beyond Boundaries

Amelia Earhart, the legendary aviator, is an exceptional case study of a woman who fearlessly embraced courage to become more confident and assertive in her professional and personal life. Born in 1897, Amelia was determined to defy societal norms and pursue her passion for aviation, a field predominantly dominated by men during her time.

## *Professional Courage*

From an early age, Amelia displayed a deep fascination with flying. In 1923, she took her first flight, an experience that forever changed her life. Undeterred by the prevailing gender norms, Amelia courageously ventured into aviation, becoming the 16th woman to be issued a pilot's license. She continuously challenged herself, setting records and breaking barriers for female aviators. 1928 she became the first woman to fly across the Atlantic Ocean. This achievement garnered widespread acclaim and solidified her reputation as a trailblazer in aviation.

Amelia's unwavering courage propelled her to attempt even bolder feats. In 1932, she achieved another milestone by becoming the first woman to fly solo across the Atlantic. Despite facing numerous challenges and skepticism, she remained steadfast in pursuing adventure and excellence.

## Personal Courage

Amelia's courage extended far beyond her professional achievements. In her personal life, she advocated for gender equality, challenging traditional roles for women and inspiring countless individuals to follow their dreams. Amelia became an iconic symbol of women's empowerment through her bold actions and outspoken nature, proving that fearlessness and assertiveness could lead to limitless possibilities.

## Facing Fears & The Ultimate Journey

In 1937, Amelia embarked on her most daring and fateful adventure – an attempt to fly around the world. Although the journey was fraught with risks and uncertainties, Amelia was undeterred. Tragically, during the final leg of her trip, her plane disappeared over the Pacific Ocean, and she was declared lost at sea.

While her ultimate fate remains a mystery, Amelia's legacy as a courageous and assertive woman endures. Her remarkable journey and fearlessness inspire generations of women to challenge societal norms, embrace courage, and strive for greatness.

## Lessons In Courage

Amelia Earhart's story offers invaluable lessons on embracing the courage to cultivate confidence and assertiveness:

- **Embrace fear as fuel:** Amelia didn't let fear paralyze her; instead, she used it as a driving force to conquer challenges. By recognizing fear as an opportunity for growth, she transformed it into fuel for her audacious pursuits.

- **Challenge gender norms:** In a male-dominated field, Amelia didn't conform to societal expectations. She courageously followed her passion, defying gender norms and empowering women worldwide to pursue their aspirations without hesitation.

- **Resilience in the face of setbacks:** Amelia faced setbacks and failures throughout her career. However, she never allowed these obstacles to deter her. Instead, she embraced resilience and determination, pushing forward with unwavering resolve.

The story of Amelia Earhart illustrates that courage is not the absence of fear but rather the willingness to act despite it. Her audacity to venture beyond the boundaries set for women during her time is a timeless reminder that courage paves the way to self-assurance, empowerment, and unyielding assertiveness. As we draw inspiration from her journey, let us remember that within each of us lies the potential to conquer fear, embrace courage, and soar to new heights of confidence and assertiveness.

## Incorporating Courage Into Your Journey

As you explore these strategies, remember that courage is not a single act but a continuous practice—a journey of self-discovery and empowerment. Each step you take towards embracing courage will build upon the previous one, creating a powerful momentum that leads to increased confidence and assertiveness.

You will unlock the wellspring of courage within you through vulnerability, challenging limiting beliefs, stepping out of your comfort zone, cultivating a growth mindset, seeking support, and practicing mindfulness and self-compassion.

As we continue our expedition into the world of courage, let us draw inspiration from the stories of courageous women who have defied the odds and made a lasting impact. Their journeys remind us that courage is not reserved for the extraordinary; it resides within each of us, waiting to be unleashed.

So, dear reader, let us embrace courage as our guiding light, propelling us forward on the path to becoming confident, assertive, and unstoppable in pursuit of our dreams. Together, we will rise above fear, shatter barriers, and embrace the limitless possibilities that lie ahead.

## Up Next?

You have now delved into the life-changing power of courage and its profound impact on becoming a more confident woman. You explored strategies to embrace courage, challenge limiting beliefs, step out of your comfort zone, seek support and inspiration, and practice mindfulness and self-compassion. By daring to embrace courage, you open doors to new possibilities, reshape your brain pathways and cultivate unshakable confidence.

As you continue your journey towards greater assertiveness, the next part of this book will focus on increasing your assertiveness in real-life experiences. In Chapter 9, we will explore how to apply the principles of assertiveness in your personal life and at home. You will discover effective communication techniques, setting boundaries, and nurturing meaningful relationships with confidence and authenticity.

# Part 3 — From Theory To Practice: Unleash Your Voice — Real-Life Mastery Of Assertiveness

# Chapter 9: Embracing Assertiveness In Diverse Realms — Empowering Your Voice & Creating Harmonious Personal Bonds

In this chapter, you will embark on a journey to empower your voice and nurture harmonious bonds.

Assertiveness is a potent communication skill, a beacon guiding you to express your needs, thoughts, and boundaries with clarity and confidence while valuing the rights and opinions of others. Prepare to uncover the art of assertiveness and its transformative potential in various personal life scenarios.

Within the following sections, you'll discover the intricacies of assertiveness at home, among friends, family, and acquaintances. Clasp the wisdom of knowing when and how to assert yourself gracefully, fostering deeper connections and mutual understanding in every interaction.

Are you ready to unlock the power of your voice, harmonize your bonds, and navigate life's diverse scenarios with confidence and grace? Let's begin arming you with the tools to embrace assertiveness with poise and authenticity.

## Assertiveness At Home: Building Harmonious Bonds

Embracing assertiveness within the comfort of home is essential for fostering open communication and building harmonious bonds among family members and friends.

Home, where we find solace and share our joys and sorrows, is the foundation of our emotional well-being.

It is a place where our relationships flourish, and we can be ourselves. Yet, it is also a space where misunderstandings and conflicts can arise, often due to unexpressed needs and boundaries.

Embracing assertiveness at home does not mean creating an environment of constant confrontation; instead, it involves cultivating a communication style that allows you to express your thoughts, feelings, and needs with clarity and respect while also valuing the opinions and emotions of others. When nurtured at home, assertiveness sets the stage for healthier and more fulfilling relationships, as everyone feels heard and understood.

## Compelling Reasons Why Assertiveness Should Start At Home

### Fostering Open Communication

Honest and open communication is the cornerstone of a thriving family. When family members embrace assertiveness, they create an atmosphere where everyone feels comfortable expressing their thoughts and emotions. This promotes a deeper understanding of one another and nurtures a sense of belonging.

### Strengthening Family Bonds

Family relationships are unique and complex, often filled with a shared history and deep emotions. Embracing assertiveness helps family members constructively navigate conflicts and differences, strengthening the bonds that tie them together.

## Setting Positive Examples

Healthily demonstrating assertiveness as a parent or guardian can positively influence the next generation. When children observe assertive communication within the family, they learn to express themselves effectively and respectfully, setting them up for success in future relationships.

## Resolving Conflicts

Every family encounters conflicts at some point. Embracing assertiveness allows disputes to be addressed openly and respectfully, leading to more effective resolution and preventing unresolved issues from simmering beneath the surface.

## Establishing Healthy Boundaries

Assertiveness empowers you to set and maintain healthy boundaries with family members. This ensures that your needs and values are respected, preventing feelings of resentment and fostering a supportive and caring environment.

# • Highly Effective Methods For Being Assertive At Home

## *Workable Compromise*

Is the practice of finding middle-ground solutions during family discussions. This allows everyone's needs to be considered and creates a sense of cooperation.

### *Example*

*Meet Sarah and Alex, a married couple with differing approaches to spending their weekends. Sarah enjoys spending quality time with friends and family, often attending gatherings and social events. On the other hand, Alex prefers relaxing at home and indulging in hobbies like reading and gardening. This difference in preferences led to occasional conflicts, with Sarah feeling disappointed when Alex declined invitations. However, Alex was left feeling overwhelmed when faced with multiple social commitments.*

*One weekend, the couple decided to discuss this issue openly. They sat down and expressed their feelings, understanding that both perspectives were valid. Sarah wanted to maintain their social connections, and Alex sought moments of relaxation and solitude. Instead of arguing, they found a workable compromise to honor their needs.*

## Steps for Finding a Workable Compromise

- *Initiate open conversation:* Schedule a time to talk calmly and respectfully about conflicting preferences or needs. Ensure that both partners feel comfortable expressing their feelings without judgment.

- *Listen actively:* Give each other your undivided attention when discussing the matter. Be empathetic and genuinely listen to the reasons behind your partner's preferences.

- *Acknowledge differences:* Recognize that each person is unique, and it's natural to have different needs and preferences. Avoid labeling one preference as better than the other.

- *Identify common ground:* Look for areas where your preferences align or overlap. It could be as simple as choosing specific weekends for social events and others for relaxation.

- *Brainstorm solutions:* Together, brainstorm various solutions that cater to both preferences. Be open to creative ideas and alternatives you may not have considered.

- *Evaluate Pros and Cons:* Assess the advantages and disadvantages of each solution. Consider the impact on your relationship and individual well-being.

- *Choose the workable compromise:* Select the most comfortable solution for both partners. It should honor the needs of both individuals and foster a sense of cooperation.

- *Set boundaries and flexibility:* Establish clear boundaries and expectations within the compromise. Allow room for flexibility and adjustments as needed in the future.

- *Commit to the compromise:* Commit to it wholeheartedly once you agree on a workable compromise. Support each other in adhering to the agreed-upon plan.

In Sarah and Alex's case, they dedicated two monthly weekends to social events and other weekends to relaxation. They also included occasional activities they both enjoyed, like cooking together or going for nature walks. This compromise allowed them to balance their social lives with moments of tranquility, deepening their understanding of one another and strengthening their relationship.

By following these steps and being open to finding a workable compromise, you can navigate conflicts with understanding and respect, enhancing the harmony in your relationships. Remember, compromise doesn't mean sacrificing your needs but instead finding a middle ground that respects the unique perspectives of both individuals.

## Keeping Emotions In Check

While emotions are valid, practice expressing them calmly and constructively. Avoid letting emotions escalate into heated arguments.

### Example

*Let's meet Jenna, a mother of two young children juggling her career and family life. One evening, after a long and tiring day, Jenna's children began to quarrel over a toy. The noise and tension escalated, and Jenna felt her frustration building up. She wanted to snap at her kids but knew an impulsive reaction wouldn't be helpful. Instead, she took a deep breath, counted to ten, and reminded herself that yelling wouldn't resolve the issue. Jenna addressed the situation calmly and talked to her children about sharing and taking turns. Jenna created a more peaceful atmosphere at home by keeping her emotions in check. She taught her children valuable lessons about conflict resolution.*

### Steps For Keeping Emotions In Check

- *Recognize triggers:* Pay attention to the situations or circumstances that trigger strong emotional reactions. Understanding your triggers empowers you to respond more thoughtfully.

- *Pause and breathe:* When you feel your emotions escalating, take a moment to pause and take deep breaths. Breathing helps you regain composure and approach the situation with a clear mind.

- *Assess the situation:* Step back and assess the situation objectively. Ask yourself if your emotions are proportionate to the issue at hand.

- *Model emotional regulation:* If you have children, remember they observe and learn from your behavior. By modeling emotional regulation, you show them how to handle emotions constructively.

- *Practice empathy:* Put yourself in the other person's shoes, even if it's your child. Understanding their feelings and perspectives can lead to more compassionate responses.

- *Choose your response:* Instead of reacting impulsively, consciously choose your comeback. Consider what approach will be most effective in addressing the situation positively.

- *Communicate clearly:* Use clear and concise language when expressing your feelings and needs. Avoid blaming or shaming language.

- *Set boundaries:* Establishing boundaries is essential for maintaining emotional balance. Know when to say no and communicate your limits respectfully.

- *Seek support:* Reach out to friends, family, or support groups when you need to vent or seek advice. Sometimes talking through your emotions can provide valuable insights.

- *Practice self-compassion:* Be kind to yourself and acknowledge that everyone experiences emotional challenges. Treat yourself with the same understanding and compassion you'd offer a friend.

By following these steps, Jenna managed to create a more nurturing and harmonious environment at home. She taught her children the importance of expressing emotions calmly and resolving conflicts peacefully. Remember, keeping emotions in check is an ongoing practice that can transform your personal relationships and lead to a more balanced and assertive life.

## Staying Calm During Conflicts

In times of conflict, take deep breaths and maintain composure. This enables you to communicate assertively without aggression.

### Example

*Meet Dave and Emily, a married couple who are both passionate and strong-willed. One day, they found themselves in a heated argument about how to manage household responsibilities. The disagreement quickly turned into a full-blown conflict, with emotions running high. In the past, such conflicts often led to shouting matches and hurt feelings.*

*However, this time was different. Dave and Emily had been working on their communication and assertiveness skills. Amid the conflict, Emily recognized that they were both overwhelmed by their emotions. Instead of escalating the situation, she took a deep breath and suggested a short break to cool off. Both agreed to step away for a few minutes.*

*During the break, they practiced calming techniques they had learned together. Emily went for a short walk to clear her mind while Dave listened to calming music. After the break, they returned to the discussion with a more level-headed approach. They took turns expressing their viewpoints, actively listening to each other, and seeking common ground. By staying calm and composed, they navigated the conflict with respect and understanding, ultimately finding a workable compromise that satisfied them both.*

## Steps for Staying Calm During Conflicts

- *Recognize escalating emotions:* Be aware of the signs, such as increased heart rate, tension, or irritability. Acknowledging these signs can help you intervene before things get out of control.

- *Take a break if needed:* If you feel overwhelmed during a conflict, suggest taking a short break to regain composure. Stepping away from the situation allows you to collect your thoughts and emotions.

- *Practice calming techniques:* Find calming techniques that work for you, such as deep breathing, meditation, or physical activity. Using these strategies during a break can help you return to the conversation with a calmer mindset.

- *Focus on listening:* During conflicts, it's essential to actively listen to the other person's perspective. Avoid interrupting and genuinely try to understand their point of view.

- *Avoid blame and accusations:* Instead of placing blame or making accusatory statements, use "I" statements to express how you feel and what you need from the other person.

- *Seek common ground:* Look for areas of agreement and shared interests. Finding common ground can pave the way for a resolution that satisfies both parties.

- *Stay respectful:* Even in the heat of the moment, maintain respect for the other person. Avoid personal attacks and stay focused on the issue at hand.

- *Keep the big picture in mind:* Remember the bigger picture and the importance of maintaining a healthy relationship. This can help you prioritize resolution over winning the argument.

- *Know when to seek support:* If conflicts become too challenging to handle on your own, consider seeking the help of a therapist or counselor. Professional support can provide valuable insights and guidance.

- *Practice patience and forgiveness:* Conflict resolution takes time and effort. Be patient with yourself and the other person, and be willing to forgive past mistakes to move forward positively.

Staying calm during conflicts creates a conducive environment for open communication and understanding. Remember, conflicts are a natural part of relationships, but how you handle them can make all the difference in building more robust and assertive connections with others.

## Understanding & Accepting Differences

Embrace the diversity within your family and strive to understand and accept each member's unique perspective and preferences.

### Example

*Sam and Maya have been close friends since childhood. They come from different cultural backgrounds, and while they share many common interests, some aspects of their lives are pretty distinct. For instance, Sam's family traditions involve large gatherings during festivals, while Maya's family prefers smaller, intimate celebrations.*

*One day, as they planned a holiday trip together, they realized their travel preferences differed. Sam loved adventure and exploring off-the-beaten-path destinations, while Maya preferred a more relaxed vacation in a comfortable resort by the beach.*

*Instead of letting these differences create tension, they approached the situation assertively. They openly communicated their preferences, listened to each other's reasons, and sought to understand the underlying motivations. Sam expressed how adventure fueled his sense of exploration, while Maya emphasized the value of relaxation to recharge her energy.*

## Steps For Understanding & Accepting Differences

- *Open communication:* Start by initiating an open and honest conversation with the person you have differences with. Create a safe space for both of you to express your thoughts and feelings without judgment.

- *Active listening:* Listen actively and attentively to the other person's perspective. Avoid interrupting and allow them to fully share their thoughts and emotions.

- *Seek understanding:* Ask questions to better understand the reasons behind their preferences or viewpoints. Show genuine curiosity and empathy towards their experiences.

- *Identify common ground:* Look for areas where your preferences align or where you can find a compromise that benefits both parties.

- *Respectful acknowledgment:* Even if you don't fully agree with the other person's viewpoint, acknowledge and respect their right to have their own preferences and opinions.

- *Value differences:* Recognize that diversity enriches our lives and broadens our horizons. Embrace the opportunity to learn from someone with different perspectives and experiences.

- *Avoid judgment:* Refrain from judging the other person's choices or beliefs. Instead, focus on building a connection based on mutual respect and understanding.

By understanding and accepting their differences, Sam and Maya could plan a trip incorporating elements of adventure and relaxation, ensuring that both could enjoy the vacation to the fullest.

Remember, embracing differences enhances our relationships, fosters personal growth, and enriches our lives with new insights and experiences.

## Using Negative Assertion

Let's explore negative assertion, a powerful technique for setting boundaries while maintaining respect for yourself and others. Negative assertion involves saying "no" or expressing disagreement firmly yet respectfully.

*Example*

*Your friend Sienna frequently asks you to accompany her to social events even when you need some alone time. You value your friendship and want to be supportive. Still, Sienna's requests are becoming overwhelming, affecting your personal space and well-being. You decide to use negative assertions to address the situation.*

## Steps For Using Negative Assertion

- *Choose the right time and place:* Find a suitable time and private space to discuss the issue with your friend. Avoid discussing it in front of others to maintain confidentiality and respect.

- *Be clear and direct:* When talking to your friend, use clear and plain language to express your feelings and boundaries. Avoid using vague language that may be open to misinterpretation.

- *Express gratitude first:* Begin by expressing gratitude for your friendship and willingness to be there for her in the past. This sets a positive tone for the conversation.

- *State your boundaries:* Politely but firmly let your friend know that you sometimes need time for yourself and cannot always attend social events. Explain that it's essential for you to maintain a healthy balance between socializing and personal time.

- *Avoid over-apologizing:* While feeling empathetic is natural, avoid over-apologizing or excessively justifying your decision. Remember that setting boundaries is essential for your well-being.

- *Offer alternatives (optional):* If you feel comfortable, you can suggest other ways you can support your friend without compromising your personal time. This shows that you still value friendship and are willing to help within your limits.

Using negative assertions, you communicated your boundaries to Sienna while maintaining respect for yourself and your friend. This approach allows you to protect your well-being and maintain a healthy balance between your personal and social life.

Remember, negative assertion is not about being harsh or uncaring; it's about respecting your needs and limitations while valuing your relationships with others. By implementing negative assertion with kindness and clarity, you can build healthier and more authentic connections in your personal life.

### Using Empathy

Empathy is a powerful tool for enhancing communication and building stronger connections with our loved ones. When you approach conversations with empathy, you show genuine understanding and concern for the emotions and experiences of the people you care about.

*Example*

*Your close friend Lisa has been acting distant and withdrawn lately. Instead of assuming she's simply in a bad mood, you approach her empathetically. You invite her for a walk in the park and create a safe space for her to share her thoughts and feelings.*

## Steps For Using Empathy

- *Choose the right moment:* Find a moment when both have free time and can have an uninterrupted conversation. Respect her boundaries and tell her you're there whenever she's ready to talk.

- *Create a safe and comfortable environment:* Opt for a relaxed setting, like a park, where your friend can feel at ease sharing her thoughts. Be approachable, and maintain an open posture to show your receptiveness.

- *Listen actively:* As your friend shares her feelings, focus on listening attentively. Avoid interrupting or jumping to conclusions. Allow her to express herself without judgment.

- *Reflect her emotions:* Acknowledge her emotions by using phrases like "It seems like you're feeling..." or "I can understand why that would make you feel...". This demonstrates that you genuinely want to understand her perspective.

- *Ask clarifying questions:* If something is unclear or you need more context, ask open-ended questions to gain further insights and show interest in her experiences.

- *Avoid making it about you:* Resist the temptation to share your own experiences unless your friend explicitly asks for your input.

- *Offer support and validation:* Let your friend know that her feelings are valid and that you appreciate her opening up. Offer your help if she needs it.

- *Respect her boundaries:* If your friend becomes uncomfortable sharing specific details or decides not to discuss certain topics, respect her decision. Reiterate that you're there for her whenever she's ready to talk.

By using empathy, you provided Lisa with the space and understanding she needed to share her feelings, which is a crucial aspect of assertiveness. Your empathetic approach demonstrated your ability to be attuned to her emotions and experiences, creating a safe environment for open communication. This strengthened your bond and showcased how assertiveness goes hand in hand with compassion and genuine care for others.

As you practice empathy in your personal relationships, you'll find that it strengthens your connections and enhances your assertiveness skills. Understanding the feelings and perspectives of those around you empowers you to express yourself assertively with greater sensitivity and consideration for others' feelings.

Remember, empathy is a powerful way to build deeper connections with your loved ones and complement and reinforce your assertiveness, making it an even more effective and compassionate communication tool.

By embracing assertiveness at home, you can create a supportive and loving environment where everyone's voice is valued. In the upcoming sections, we will explore assertiveness in other areas of life, including the workplace and challenging social situations. Building harmonious bonds at home lays the foundation for confidently asserting yourself in all aspects of life. So, let's continue on this empowering journey of assertiveness together, unlocking the full potential of your relationships and personal growth.

# Assertiveness With Friends & Acquaintances: Nurturing Authentic Connections & Navigating New Ones

Friendships are the bedrock of support and camaraderie. Embracing assertiveness with friends nurtures genuine connections and encourages open communication. In social settings, assertiveness helps navigate interactions with acquaintances, setting the foundation for potential future friendships.

## 7 Tips For Assertiveness With Friends & Acquaintances

1. **Polite declines:** When declining an invitation or request, respond assertively yet politely, explaining your reasons without feeling obligated to provide excessive details.

2. **Small talk with purpose:** Engage in small talk with acquaintances, expressing genuine interest in their lives. Assertiveness allows you to create meaningful connections beyond superficial interactions.

3. **Holding boundaries:** Maintain personal boundaries in social settings, asserting yourself when necessary to protect your comfort and well-being.

4. **Positive inquiry:** When receiving compliments, embrace the power of positive inquiry. Instead of brushing off the compliment, ask your friend to elaborate on what they liked about your actions or accomplishments.

5. **Giving and receiving criticism:** Approach constructive criticism with an open mind, focusing on growth rather than taking it personally. Be honest yet respectful when providing feedback, ensuring your words empower rather than belittle.

6. **Embracing vulnerability:** Allow yourself to be vulnerable with your friends by authentically sharing your thoughts and feelings. Vulnerability fosters deeper connections and demonstrates trust in your friendships.

7. **Negative inquiry:** When faced with criticism from acquaintances, practice "negative inquiry" by asking for clarification on their concerns. Seek to understand their perspective without becoming defensive.

Embracing assertiveness is a decisive step towards fostering authentic communication and empowering yourself in every aspect of life. As you navigate interactions with grace, empathy, and confidence, you will witness the transformation of your relationships and the unfolding of new opportunities. By applying the tips and strategies mentioned in this chapter, you will find that assertiveness becomes a natural and indispensable part of your daily life.

However, assertiveness isn't limited to comfortable situations alone. Life often presents us with challenging moments where staying true to our needs and boundaries may seem daunting. In the next section, we will explore strategies for embracing assertiveness in uncomfortable situations, allowing you to navigate demanding or manipulative individuals, constructively give and receive criticism, and even gracefully accept compliments.

### *Up Next?*

This chapter delved into the art of assertiveness in various personal life scenarios. It revealed how assertiveness enhances communication by allowing you to express your needs while respecting others' opinions. You explored applying assertiveness at home, among friends, family, and acquaintances. From fostering open communication to understanding and accepting differences, you have learned to nurture harmonious relationships.

This chapter equipped you with essential strategies to embrace assertiveness, setting the stage for the upcoming exploration of handling uncomfortable situations in Chapter 10. Get ready to delve deep into the art of assertively handling challenging situations and dealing with manipulative individuals. Discover strategies to maintain your voice and boundaries when faced with demanding scenarios. You'll explore techniques to give and receive criticism constructively, ensuring personal growth and improved relationships. I will also guide you on gracefully accepting compliments while staying humble. Prepare to fortify your assertiveness skills and navigate life's complexities confidently and authentically.

# Chapter 10: Unleashing Your Assertive Voice: Embracing Challenging Situations With Confidence

In the pursuit of mastering assertiveness, this chapter will guide you to tackling life's most challenging scenarios with unwavering confidence. From dealing with demanding and manipulative individuals to gracefully receiving criticism and compliments, you'll learn the art of assertive communication that ensures your voice is heard while respecting others. Dive into the D.E.S.C. model for navigating conflicts and discover the cathartic potential of "I" statements. By embracing these techniques, you'll navigate the complexities of relationships and conflicts and uncover the essence of assertive strength within you. So, gear up to convert your communication, as this chapter equips you to emerge from challenging situations with newfound confidence and grace.

# Dealing With Demanding Or Manipulative Individuals

It can be incredibly challenging to deal with demanding or manipulative individuals due to the emotional toll it takes on us. Such individuals may use aggressive tactics or emotional manipulation to pressure us into complying with their wishes. They might undermine our confidence, making us doubt our judgment and decisions. Moreover, their relentless persistence and disregard for our boundaries can leave us feeling trapped and disempowered, impacting our self-esteem and overall well-being.

To handle such challenging situations with confidence and assertiveness, equipping ourselves with effective strategies such as the following is essential:

### *Fogging*

Practicing "fogging" can be a powerful approach when faced with unreasonable demands or manipulation. Fogging involves responding calmly and non-confrontational, acknowledging the person's demands without fully committing to them. By using phrases like, "I see that you want me to handle this task immediately. I'll take it into consideration and let you know when I can address it," you avoid escalating the situation while still asserting your right to make decisions at your own pace.

### Setting Clear Boundaries

Establishing and maintaining firm boundaries is crucial when dealing with demanding or manipulative individuals. Clearly communicate your limits and expectations, and be assertive in enforcing them. Standing your ground without allowing guilt or pressure to sway your decisions is essential.

### Detached Engagement

Detached engagement involves maintaining emotional distance while staying assertively engaged in the conversation. Rather than getting entangled in an antagonist's emotional manipulation, you keep your composure and respond with clear, direct communication. Detached engagement protects your emotions and mental well-being from the negative impact of their tactics, allowing you to focus on maintaining your assertiveness and boundaries.

In practice, you might respond with phrases such as, "I understand your point of view, but I must prioritize my own needs," or "I hear what you're saying, but I need some time to think things through before making a decision." By acknowledging their input without becoming emotionally involved, you retain control over the conversation and prevent their tactics from affecting your assertiveness.

Detached engagement empowers you to maintain strength and assertiveness, even under intense pressure or emotional manipulation. It sends a powerful message that you are not easily swayed and that your decisions are grounded in your values and needs.

Remember, dealing with demanding or manipulative individuals requires a blend of confidence and empathy. By implementing these strategies in your personal life, you can navigate such challenges gracefully and assertively, ultimately maintaining control over your choices and well-being.

# Giving Or Receiving Criticism

An integral part of personal and professional growth is giving and receiving criticism. Constructive criticism offers valuable insights, helping you identify areas for improvement and learn from your mistakes. On the giving end, providing feedback thoughtfully and assertively can strengthen relationships, foster growth, and promote effective communication. On the receiving end, being open to criticism allows us to gain a fresh perspective and make positive changes. However, giving and receiving criticism can be challenging, often triggering emotional responses and vulnerability. It's crucial to approach these situations assertively, balancing honest feedback and empathy.

## Strategies For Giving Criticism Assertively

- **Use "I" statements:** When giving criticism, frame your feedback using "I" statements instead of "you" statements. This approach helps avoid sounding accusatory and fosters a more constructive conversation. For example, instead of saying, "You always miss deadlines," rephrase it as, "I feel concerned when deadlines are not met because it impacts the team's progress."

- **Offer praise alongside criticism:** Balancing criticism with praise helps maintain a positive and encouraging tone. Acknowledge the person's strengths and efforts before providing feedback for improvement. This approach creates a more balanced and receptive environment for receiving constructive criticism.

## Strategies For Receiving Criticism Assertively

- **Practice "negative inquiry":** When receiving criticism, practice "negative inquiry" to gather more insights into the other person's perspective. Instead of getting defensive, ask open-ended questions like, "Can you help me understand specifically what I could have done differently?" or "What aspects of my performance should I focus on improving?" This approach shows that you are receptive to feedback and willing to work on areas of growth.

- **Responding to negative or unhelpful criticism:** When faced with adverse or unhelpful criticism, it's essential to stay composed and not react impulsively. Take a moment to process the feedback and assess its validity. If the criticism is unwarranted or does not align with your values and goals, practice assertiveness by responding calmly and confidently. You can say, "Thank you for sharing your perspective. I'll consider it, but I also believe in my approach and its effectiveness." Remember, assertiveness allows you to stand up for yourself without resorting to aggression or defensiveness.

## *Practical Approaches That Work For Both*

- **Use active listening:** Active listening is vital, whether giving or receiving criticism. When giving feedback, ensure you fully understand the other person's perspective and concerns. Avoid interrupting and allow them to express themselves completely. When receiving criticism, actively listen to the feedback without becoming defensive. Focus on understanding the underlying message and ask clarifying questions if needed.

- **Focus on specific behavior:** When criticizing, focus on specific behaviors or actions rather than generalizing about the person. Detailed feedback is more actionable and less likely to cause a defensive response. Similarly, when receiving criticism, focus on the specific feedback provided and avoid taking it as a personal attack.

- **Choose the right setting:** Consider the appropriate time and place for giving or receiving criticism. Find a comfortable private setting that allows for an open and honest conversation. Avoid giving feedback in public or high-pressure environments, as it may lead to defensiveness.

# Receiving Compliments With Grace: Hold The Sway Of Assertive Appreciation

Can you embrace the art of receiving compliments with grace and assertiveness? Like most women, you probably hate or feel uncomfortable receiving compliments because you just don't know how to act or what to reply with. If this sounds like you, then this section will help immensely. Compliments are beautiful gifts bestowed upon us by others to express appreciation, admiration, and recognition for our qualities, achievements, or efforts. When someone pays you a compliment, it reflects your positive impact on their lives or the world around you. Understanding the significance of compliments can help you embrace them wholeheartedly and respond with genuine appreciation.

## The Meaning Behind Compliments

People offer compliments as acts of kindness and encouragement. Complimenting others is a way to uplift spirits, strengthen connections, and celebrate each other's accomplishments. It fosters a positive and supportive atmosphere where individuals feel valued and acknowledged for their uniqueness and contributions. Moreover, giving compliments expresses gratitude and admiration, allowing people to share positive energy and celebrate the good in one another.

## The Challenge Of Receiving Compliments

Despite the well-intentioned nature of compliments, some may find it challenging to receive them graciously. Inner voices of self-doubt or imposter syndrome may surface, causing discomfort or disbelief. You might feel undeserving or worry about appearing boastful. However, by embracing assertiveness, you can genuinely receive praise while remaining humble and appreciative.

## Assertiveness: Your Key To Embracing Compliments

Assertiveness empowers you to accept compliments gracefully, recognizing your worth and contributions without diminishing or dismissing them. By practicing assertive appreciation, you can honor the giver's kindness while staying authentic. Assertiveness lets you acknowledge your accomplishments and receive compliments warmly without needing to downplay or deflect praise.

### *Strategies For Assertive Appreciation*

- **Accept and acknowledge effort:** When receiving a compliment, you can respond by recognizing the effort you put into the achievement being praised. For example, "Thank you, I worked hard on this project, and I'm glad it's being recognized." By highlighting your dedication and commitment, you show that compliments reflect your genuine accomplishments. When someone offers a compliment, receive it with a genuine smile and accept the praise gracefully, understanding that you deserve recognition for your efforts. Avoid the temptation to downplay your achievements or shift the focus elsewhere. By sincerely receiving compliments, you honor your accomplishments and show respect for the giver's thoughtful words.

- **Focus on impact:** Instead of getting caught up in self-doubt, focus on your actions' impact. Recognize that your efforts have made a positive difference, whether it's in your work, relationships, or personal growth. Embrace the idea that graciously accepting compliments allows you to receive positive reinforcement and fuels your motivation to continue making a meaningful impact.

- **Share credit:** If applicable, it's okay to acknowledge the teamwork or collaboration that contributed to your success. Express gratitude by saying, "Thank you. This achievement wouldn't have been possible without the support of my team." Sharing credit demonstrates humility and an understanding of the collective effort that goes into accomplishments.

- **Connect with emotions:** Allow yourself to connect emotionally with the compliment. Express genuine gratitude and share your feelings, such as, "I'm truly touched by your words. Your encouragement means a lot to me." This authentic response deepens the connection between you and the giver.

- **Positive inquiry:** If you find it challenging to accept a compliment, turn it into an opportunity for positive inquiry. Respond to the praise with curiosity and appreciation by asking questions such as, "Thank you for your kind words. Can you tell me what specific aspect you liked?" By seeking more details, you show genuine interest in the compliment and internalize it with greater clarity.

Accepting compliments with grace and assertiveness doesn't make you arrogant or boastful. It's a powerful display of self-awareness and self-respect, acknowledging your worth without seeking validation from others. By embracing assertiveness in the face of compliments, you create a positive cycle of appreciation, kindness, and celebration, fostering deeper connections and uplifting the spirits of those around you. So, stand tall, accept the praise with open arms, and let the warm glow of compliments enhance your journey of self-discovery and personal growth toward your ultimate goal of increased executive presence.

# Approaches For Navigating Conflicts Assertively

## • The D.E.S.C. Model

Conflicts are a natural part of life, but how you handle them can significantly impact the outcome. The D.E.S.C. conflict resolution model provides a clear and effective structure to address conflicts while maintaining assertiveness. By following these steps, you can navigate challenging situations with confidence and ensure your needs are respected:

### 1. Describe

Start by clearly describing the behavior or situation that is causing the conflict. Use specific and objective language to avoid misunderstandings. For instance, "I noticed we've been missing deadlines for the past two weeks."

### 2. Express

Express your feelings about the behavior or situation without placing blame. Use "I" statements to convey your emotions and thoughts. For example, "I feel frustrated because the missed deadlines affect our team's progress."

## 3. Specify

Be specific about the changes you want in the behavior or situation. Clearly outline your expectations and what you believe would lead to a resolution. For instance, "I suggest we set up a clear timeline and allocate tasks to prevent further delays."

## 4. Consequences

Communicate the consequences of not addressing the conflict while emphasizing the positive outcomes of resolving it. This part is not about threats but about explaining the impact of the conflict on the overall situation. For example, "If we don't address this issue, it might impact our team's credibility and hinder our project's success. However, working together to find a solution can ensure a smoother process moving forward."

### Real Life Scenario

Lately, you've noticed that your close friend Lena often cancels plans at the last minute without much explanation. It leaves you feeling disappointed and undervalued. You decide to address the issue using the D.E.S.C. model:

*Describe:* During a one-on-one conversation, you calmly describe the behavior bothering you. You say, "I've noticed that there have been a few instances where our plans have been canceled at the last minute."

*Express:* You express your feelings without blaming or accusing. "I value our friendship, and I need to be able to rely on our plans. When they're canceled suddenly, I feel let down."

*Specify:* You offer a suggestion for improvement. "I'd appreciate it if we could communicate more about our plans in advance, so we can manage our schedules better and avoid misunderstandings."

*Consequences:* You explain the positive outcomes of resolving the issue. "By addressing this, we can ensure that our time together is more meaningful and that we both feel respected and valued in our friendship."

Using the D.E.S.C. model in this personal life scenario helps you assertively communicate your feelings and expectations while maintaining the connection with your friend. You can take a proactive and structured approach to conflicts. It allows for a productive conversation and the potential for positive changes in your interactions. Remember, the goal isn't just to resolve the conflict; it's to maintain dignity and respect throughout the process. Practice using this model, and you'll find that conflicts can be opportunities for growth, collaboration, and strengthened relationships.

# • The Power of "I" Statements: Communicating Assertively & Respectfully

Assertive communication involves expressing your thoughts, feelings and needs directly and respectfully. One highly effective tool for achieving this is using "I" statements. These statements shift the focus from placing blame or making accusations to expressing your emotions and perspective. Here's why "I" statements are crucial and how to use them in real-life situations, along with a connection to the D.E.S.C. model:

## What Are "I" Statements & Why Are They Beneficial?

"I" statements are a communication technique emphasizing personal responsibility and ownership of your feelings. They provide a structured way to express yourself without causing defensiveness in others. By framing your thoughts in terms of your own emotions and experiences, you create a non-confrontational space for dialogue. This approach is fundamental when dealing with manipulative individuals or challenging situations, as it helps prevent conflict escalation and maintains open communication.

## Using "I" Statements In Real-Life Scenarios

Consider a scenario where a friend often asks you for favors but never reciprocates. Instead of resorting to blaming or confrontation, use an "I" statement to express how you feel assertively:

1. **Identify the situation:** Clearly identify the situation that is bothering you. In this case, your friend consistently asks for favors without offering help in return.

2. **Express your emotions:** State how the situation makes you feel using "I" language. For instance, say, "I feel a bit overwhelmed and unbalanced when I keep helping out without receiving the same support."

3. **Specify the behavior:** Describe the specific behavior you'd like to address. In this case, it's the lack of reciprocity in your friendship.

4. **Effect on you:** Explain how this behavior affects you. For example, say, "It's important for me to feel that our friendship is mutually supportive. When there's an imbalance, it makes me question if our relationship is truly balanced."

By using an "I" statement, you're conveying your emotions and concerns while taking ownership of your feelings. This approach encourages open dialogue and understanding, reducing the likelihood of the conversation becoming confrontational or leading to manipulation.

## Connecting "I" Statements & The D.E.S.C. Model

While both "I" statements and the D.E.S.C. model share the goal of effective communication, they approach it from slightly different angles. The D.E.S.C. model describes the situation, expresses feelings, specifies desired changes, and highlights consequences. On the other hand, "I" statements emphasize your feelings and needs while promoting open dialogue. Integrating both techniques into your communication toolkit allows you to handle challenging situations with versatility and assertiveness, ensuring your messages are heard and understood.

### Up Next?

As you've embraced assertiveness in various facets of your personal life, you've laid a solid foundation for thriving professionally. In Chapter 11, we'll delve into the dynamic arena of work scenarios, where assertiveness is crucial to your success and executive presence. From negotiating projects to voicing your opinions in meetings, you'll discover invaluable strategies to enhance your assertiveness, ensuring you make your mark in the workplace. Get ready to step into your professional prowess as you uncover the nuances of assertive communication in a work setting, transforming challenges into opportunities for growth and influence.

# Chapter 11: Amplifying Your Assertiveness In The Workplace

Welcome to the pinnacle of your assertiveness journey. As you enter the realm of the workplace, your cultivated confidence and assertiveness are set to transform into an unmistakable executive presence. This chapter is your guide to infusing your interactions with the commanding essence of a leader. It's not just about communication techniques; it's about exuding strength, clarity, and authenticity in every encounter. As you master the art of assertiveness in various scenarios – from team leadership to addressing adversity – you'll elevate your presence during job interviews, evaluations, and beyond. This isn't just about saying 'no' or handling conflicts; it's about shaping outcomes, leaving a lasting impact, and cementing yourself as an assertive and influential force in the professional arena.

## Assertiveness With Your Team: A Pillar Of Executive Presence

At the heart of executive presence lies the ability to assertively lead while inspiring your team to reach new heights. A true leader manages tasks and ignites the spark of motivation within their team, propelling them towards success. This chapter illuminates the art of assertive leadership within your team, transforming your role from mere manager to a beacon of inspiration. You'll authentically radiate executive presence by mastering the delicate balance between confidence and collaboration while fostering a dynamic and united work environment.

# Blueprints For Leadership Excellence

Embracing assertiveness in your leadership approach yields a plethora of benefits. Firstly, it forges a transparent and structured work environment where roles, expectations, and goals are unmistakably defined. This clarity is a guiding star, minimizing confusion and enhancing overall productivity. Secondly, assertive leadership exudes confidence and decisiveness, inevitably fostering a culture of respect and trust among team members. Moreover, this authoritative yet empathetic stance empowers open communication, allowing team members to comfortably share ideas and concerns, thus propelling the engine of innovation forward.

## • Constructive Feedback Redefined: Applying the L.A.D.D.E.R. Approach

A potent strategy to exercise assertiveness within your team involves utilizing the L.A.D.D.E.R. approach for delivering constructive feedback. This approach aligns harmoniously with the journey to executive presence, becoming a North Star that guides you through interactions, ensuring your message resonates with confidence and authority.

Imagine possessing a roadmap for each conversation, a roadmap that not only ensures your voice is heard but also amplifies your executive aura. The L.A.D.D.E.R. approach stands as this roadmap, a dynamic mnemonic that encapsulates the essence of assertive communication, empowering you to provide feedback constructively. L.A.D.D.E.R. stands for Listening, Assessing, Deciding, Declaring, Explaining, and Reinforcing, offering a comprehensive pathway to mastering the art of assertive communication.

## Elevating Leadership With L.A.D.D.E.R: A Step-By-Step Journey

Allow the L.A.D.D.E.R. approach to weave its magic through a real-life scenario involving Mia, a team member grappling with meeting deadlines.

### Listening

Initiate the process by actively listening to Mia's perspective. Uncover her challenges and delve into her thoughts regarding the missed deadlines. Your attentive ear isn't just an act of courtesy; it's a beacon of respect and a gateway to open communication. By genuinely understanding Mia's viewpoint, you lay the foundation of empathy.

### Assessing

The next step involves a pause for a comprehensive assessment. Contemplate the ripple effect of Mia's missed deadlines on team progress and morale. Comprehend her workload and external factors contributing to her struggles. This holistic assessment arms you with insights, enabling you to approach the conversation with a profound understanding.

### Deciding

Build on your assessment to decide how to tackle the issue. Set clear goals for the conversation – not just addressing the problem but nurturing Mia's growth. Your decision may involve a collaborative strategy that aids her improvement while maintaining team productivity.

## Declaring

With your decision in hand, articulate it assertively and transparently. Utilize a direct style of language that underscores your intention to foster Mia's development. Express your desire to discuss the missed deadlines and collectively explore pathways to overcome these challenges. This declaration sets the tone for an impactful dialogue.

## Explaining

Offer a concise explanation that sheds light on your decision. Share your observations regarding the missed deadlines and their repercussions on the team. Clarify that your objective is to find advantageous solutions for Mia and the team, bridging the gap between your assertiveness and your commitment to collaboration.

## Reinforcing

As the conversation unfolds, reinforce your dedication to Mia's growth and the team's triumph. Acknowledge her strengths and contributions while emphasizing your unwavering belief in her potential. This reinforcement nurtures a sense of self-assurance and accountability in Mia.

By seamlessly integrating the L.A.D.D.E.R. approach into your feedback conversation with Mia, you display assertive leadership and foster growth and collaboration. Your empathetic listening, comprehensive assessment, clear communication, and unwavering reinforcement paint a picture of assertiveness rooted in respect and the desire for mutual success. Through these assertive yet supportive interactions, you elevate your executive presence, solidifying your role as a leader who propels both results and the growth of your team.

# • Alternative Framework For Delivering Constructive Feedback - S.T.E.P.S.

### *Workplace Scenario*

Imagine you're a department head at a tech company. Your team is responsible for developing a groundbreaking software application crucial for a client's business expansion. Among your team members is Keira, a skilled programmer known for her innovative solutions. However, lately, her coding errors have been causing setbacks and undermining the project's progress. You decide to use the S.T.E.P.S. approach to address the problem with Keira and offer constructive feedback.

S - Setting the stage
- *Start positively:* You initiate the conversation by acknowledging Keira's expertise in coding and her track record of creative problem-solving.

- *Express intent:* With a supportive tone, you emphasize your commitment to her professional growth and the project's success. You aim to ensure her potential contributes effectively to the team's achievements.

## T - Targeted observations

- *Be specific:* You delve into the instances where coding errors led to delays, causing recalibrations and additional workload for the team.

- *Stay objective:* Your language remains neutral and objective, focusing on the technical outcomes rather than personal blame.

## E - Engage in dialogue

- *Encourage openness:* You create an atmosphere of openness, inviting Keira to share her perspective on the challenges she's encountering.

- *Listen actively:* As Keira explains her approach and difficulties, you listen attentively, ensuring she feels valued and understood.

## P - Provide solutions

- *Collaborate on solutions:* You propose brainstorming solutions together, acknowledging her technical insights as valuable contributions.

- *Set clear goals*: Collaboratively, you set specific goals for debugging processes and implementing effective coding practices, ensuring smoother collaboration within the team.

## S - Summarize & support

- *Recap the conversation:* You recap the discussed solutions, ensuring you and Keira are aligned on the strategies moving forward.

- *Offer support:* You assure Keira of your availability to provide guidance and resources, highlighting your commitment to her professional development.

In the dynamic leadership landscape, assertiveness within your team is a cornerstone of executive presence. Mastering the balance between confidence and collaboration defines your role and cultivates an environment of innovation and growth. Harnessing the power of constructive feedback through the L.A.D.D.E.R. approach empowers you to lead assertively. By listening, assessing, deciding, declaring, explaining, and reinforcing, you navigate challenges while nurturing your team's potential. Alternatively, the S.T.E.P.S. approach offers another avenue for impactful conversations. Both strategies, when skillfully applied to real-life scenarios like Mia's and Keira's, solidify your role as a leader who propels both results and the development of your team.

# Navigating Essential Work Situations With Assertiveness

In professional life, executive presence takes center stage during pivotal work situations. These moments demand a blend of confidence, finesse, and assertiveness. Whether you're presenting groundbreaking proposals or steering high-stakes meetings, your ability to navigate these scenarios with grace and determination defines your leadership. Let's explore three pivotal work situations and unravel the art of handling them assertively.

## *Presenting Game-Changing Proposals: Empowering Your Ideas*

Imagine you're a marketing director in a fast-paced ad agency. Your team has ideated a revolutionary campaign that could redefine the industry. You're slated to present the proposal to a room filled with skeptical clients and senior executives. Here's how you navigate this scenario with assertiveness:

Guide To Tackle It:

1. *Preparation is power:* Days before the presentation, delve into exhaustive research. Anticipate questions, objections, and potential concerns. Your thorough preparation is the bedrock of your assertiveness.

2. *Craft a compelling narrative:* **Build your** presentation as a story. Begin with a captivating hook that draws everyone in. State the problem, present your innovative solution, and back it up with data-driven insights.

3. *Comprise self-assurance and engagement:* **During** the presentation, maintain eye contact and exude confidence. Answer questions with well-reasoned responses. Your assertive demeanor will inspire trust in your proposal.

### Real-Life Example:

Sheryl Sandberg, C.O.O. of Facebook, adeptly navigated a critical moment when pitching the concept of boosting ad revenue through mobile platforms. With meticulous preparation and an assertive presentation style, she convinced her team to take the leap, leading to a significant business expansion.

## Leading High-Stakes Meetings: Orchestrating Unity

Picture yourself as a project manager overseeing a cross-functional team of engineers and designers. The project has hit a roadblock, and tensions are running high. Your task is to lead a meeting that aligns everyone's efforts and breaks through the impasse.

Guide To Tackle It:

1. *Set the tone early:* Open the meeting with a clear agenda and a reminder of the common goal. Acknowledge the challenges and express confidence in the team's ability to overcome them.

2. *Foster inclusive dialogue:* Encourage team members to share their insights and concerns. Create an environment where diverse perspectives are respected, reinforcing your assertive leadership.

3. *Direct the discussion:* Steer the conversation towards common ground in the face of conflicting opinions. Highlight areas of agreement and outline actionable steps forward.

Real-Life Example:

Indra Nooyi, former C.E.O. of PepsiCo, exemplified assertiveness by leading her team by introducing healthier product options. She transformed potentially contentious meetings into collaborative platforms, ensuring a united strategy aligned with shifting consumer preferences.

## Managing Conflicts With Clients: Diplomacy & Resoluteness

Visualize yourself as a senior consultant at a prestigious law firm. You've encountered resistance from a high-profile client regarding the legal strategy. The client's expectations clash with your legal insights, and you must resolve the situation while maintaining the client's trust.

## Guide To Tackle It:

1. *Listen intently:* When the client voices concerns, actively listen without interrupting. Show genuine interest in understanding their perspective, reinforcing your commitment to a productive dialogue.

2. *Clarify and educate:* Articulate your viewpoint with clarity, backing it up with legal precedents and logical reasoning. Educate the client about the rationale behind your strategy.

3. *Find common ground:* Seek areas of agreement and build on them. Emphasize shared goals and the client's best interests while integrating your expertise into the solution.

## Real-Life Example:

Ruth Bader Ginsburg, former Supreme Court Associate Justice, exhibited remarkable assertiveness when engaging with attorneys during oral arguments. She would interrupt long-winded arguments to pose pointed questions, guiding the conversation toward the heart of the case and ensuring a thorough exploration of legal issues.

These pivotal work situations serve as litmus tests in the tapestry of executive presence. The ability to wield assertiveness and strategic finesse becomes your armor. As you channel the assertive spirits of trailblazers like Sheryl Sandberg, Indra Nooyi, and Ruth Bader Ginsburg, you weave your own narrative of leadership excellence. Through each presentation, meeting, and conflict resolution, you reaffirm your role as a guiding force, radiating an aura of influence and decisiveness.

# Saying No & Setting Boundaries: A Foundation Of Executive Presence

In the intricate sketching out of professional life, learning to say "no" and assertively establish boundaries is akin to creating the framework for a modern-day masterpiece. These skills are the keystones of executive presence and guardians of your time and priorities. Imagine sculpting your work-life canvas with unwavering strokes, creating a masterpiece of self-assured composure and unyielding control.

### Nurturing The Power Of Assertive "No"

Meet Alexa, a driven sales manager known for her commitment to her team's success. Amidst a tight schedule, a colleague approaches her with a request to assist in a non-essential project. The moment encapsulates the essence of assertive boundary-setting: gracefully declining while preserving professional rapport.

## Steps To Mastering The Art Of "No"

1. *Pause and evaluate:* Before responding, take a mindful pause to assess the request's alignment with your current workload and priorities.

2. *Express gratitude:* Begin with an appreciation for being considered, highlighting your respect for the colleague's choice of you.

3. *Direct and clear decline:* Politely decline the request while explaining that your current commitments prevent you from offering the attention the task deserves.

4. *Suggest viable alternatives:* If feasible, propose alternative solutions, such as referring another colleague who may be available or suggesting a more suitable timeframe for your involvement.

5. *Preserve professionalism:* Craft your response with a respectful and professional tone. Assertive doesn't necessitate apologetic.

### Illustration From Reality

Oprah Winfrey, a luminary in media and communication, has mastered the graceful "no" while staying true to her vision. Oprah gracefully declines when faced with requests beyond her capacity, exemplifying the art of preserving her commitments. For instance, she once refused an invitation to a high-profile event due to her prior commitments to her philanthropic initiatives. She demonstrated the power of saying "no" with grace and conviction, staying aligned with her priorities and values.

## Boundaries: Fortifying Your Work Ecosystem

Step into Cassy's shoes, a project lead in a bustling tech startup. Her imaginative prowess flourishes when immersed in focused tasks, yet frequent disruptions hamper her creative flow. The story of Cassy reveals the power of setting boundaries as a shield against interruptions.

A Guiding Path To Boundary Setting:

1. *Define your time and space:* Cassy excels by defining her focused work hours. She recognizes that her mornings and late afternoons are prime time for undistracted productivity. Using a shared calendar, she blocks these periods, sending a clear signal to her team about her dedicated work zones.

2. *Open dialogue clearly:* Cassy sets the stage for effective collaboration during daily morning briefings. She openly communicates her boundaries, emphasizing her dedication to their

collective goals. This fosters transparency and creates a space for her team to respect her focused time, setting the tone for respectful interactions.

3. *Offer collaborative solutions:* Cassy's knack for collaboration shines through her inventive solutions. She proposes "office hours" slots for in-depth discussions, allowing team members to address non-urgent matters without disrupting her workflow. Additionally, she champions using project management software for queries, ensuring that essential questions are addressed in a structured and organized manner.

4. *Stand by your principles:* Cassy's commitment to her boundaries remains unwavering. When colleagues approach during her designated focused hours, she greets them with a warm smile and a gentle reminder of her dedicated work time. This firm yet friendly approach reinforces that her workspace is sacred for focused tasks.

As you journey through the landscape of executive presence, the mastery of saying "no" and setting boundaries becomes your armor of authenticity and control. By embodying the art of assertive refusal and crafting well-defined boundaries like Cassy, you curate an environment where your professional persona exudes unwavering strength, focus, and self-assured leadership.

Sara Blakely, the founder of Spanx and a prominent entrepreneur, also recognizes the significance of boundaries. She carves out "deep work" periods in her schedule to maintain her creative edge and strategic focus, reflecting the importance of fortifying borders for optimal productivity.

Embarking on the journey of executive presence, you wield the brushes of assertive "no" and boundary-setting to craft a self-assured and dynamic canvas. With each graceful decline and every steadfast boundary, you paint a portrait of a professional who values their time, illuminating a path toward undiluted composure and unwavering control. Like Oprah Winfrey and Sara Blakely, you become the master of your narrative, fostering authenticity and strength in your professional artwork.

# The Transformative Power Of Assertive Verbs: Crafting Impactful Communication

Language is a potent instrument in asserting your presence, with the choice of verbs playing a pivotal role. Assertive verbs infuse your communication with clarity, determination, and a sense of ownership. They propel your messages from passive to commanding, leaving a lasting impact on your audience.

## Empower Your Communication With Assertive Verbs

Assertive verbs transcend mere language; they sculpt your ideas into powerful statements that demand attention. By using these verbs, you bridge the gap between intention and impact. Your communication becomes a forceful instrument for change, enabling you to inspire action, present solutions, and drive decisions.

Whether presenting ideas, leading discussions, or negotiating terms, strategically using assertive verbs is your gateway to influential communication. Just as influential female leaders like Condoleezza Rice and Hillary Clinton harnessed the might of powerful verbs to shape history, you, too, can transform your communication into a symphony of conviction, leaving a legacy of impactful influence in your professional journey.

## How To Elevate Your Message Through Assertive Verbs

Imagine you're leading a pivotal presentation to pitch your team's innovative project to potential investors. Your choice of verbs can either elevate your proposal to a compelling narrative or relegate it to a mundane account. Here's how harnessing assertive verbs can reshape your communication:

- **The power of certainty:** When you use assertive verbs, you inject a sense of certainty into your message. Instead of saying, "We might explore new strategies," assertively declare, "We will explore innovative strategies to drive success." Much like Condoleezza Rice, who firmly asserted during her tenure as Secretary of State, "We will confront threats to America's national security with determination and strength."

- **Commanding action:** Assertive verbs are action-oriented, propelling your audience to take notice and engage. Transform passive language like "There might be improvements" into an active and decisive language such as "Let's initiate improvements for enhanced outcomes." This echoed Hilary Clinton's statement: "We will work tirelessly to bring about positive change."

- **Inspiring confidence:** Using assertive verbs reflects your confidence in your ideas. By saying, "We believe this approach will yield substantial results," you project assurance in your proposal's potential. Similar to Condoleezza Rice's confident declaration that, "We will continue to lead with conviction."

- **Fostering ownership:** Assertive verbs impart a sense of ownership and responsibility to your communication. Instead of stating, "Changes might be made," declare, "We will take the necessary steps to implement these changes." Hilary Clinton exemplified this by saying, "We will take control of our future."

- **Cutting through ambiguity:** Assertive verbs eliminate ambiguity, leaving no room for misinterpretation. When you state, "This action will lead to cost savings," your message becomes crystal clear. Much like Condoleezza Rice's direct assertion, "We will not tolerate any threats to our security."

- **Influencing decisions:** Your choice of verbs can influence decision-making. An assertive "We recommend" carries more weight than a passive "We suggest." This aligns with Hilary Clinton's approach when she emphasized, "We recommend immediate action."

- **Commanding attention:** Assertive verbs captivate attention and underscore the importance of your points. Compare the impact of, "This innovation demands immediate attention" to, "This innovation might deserve attention." Condoleezza Rice once demanded attention when she stated, "We demand progress."

- **Demonstrating leadership:** Assertive verbs mirror your leadership presence. Instead of saying, "I hope we can achieve our goals," assertively state, "I am confident we will achieve our goals." Hilary Clinton's confident assertion, "We are committed to leading the way," exemplifies this.

# Mastering Adept Negotiation Skills: Navigating Toward Executive Presence

Picture yourself in a high-stakes scenario: You're at the negotiation table, advocating for a critical project's resources and support. Your ability to negotiate adeptly is not just a tactical skill; it's a powerful avenue to solidify your executive presence. Effective negotiation hinges on your confidence, assertiveness, and strategic finesse. As you delve into the world of negotiation, you're not just shaping deals – you're crafting your path to becoming an influential leader.

### *The Significance Of Adept Negotiation Skills*

In your journey toward executive presence, adept negotiation skills are like the navigator of your ship. They empower you to steer through complex waters with finesse, securing the best possible outcomes for yourself, your team, and your organization. Here I outline for you why mastering negotiation is pivotal for ensuring your executive presence:

- **Building resilience:** Effective negotiation demands robust self-assurance. When you navigate the ebb and flow of discussions, adapting to shifting dynamics, you showcase resilience. This resilience is a cornerstone of executive presence, demonstrating your ability to stand firm in the face of challenges.

- **Fostering collaboration:** Negotiation is not a battle but a collaborative dance of interests. Your adeptness at negotiation fosters an environment of cooperation where parties work together for mutual benefit. This collaborative spirit mirrors the essence of executive presence, showcasing your capacity to unite diverse perspectives for collective growth.

- **Exuding confidence:** Effective negotiation is a reflection of your self-confidence. As you articulate your position with clarity and poise, you radiate an aura of confidence – a quality integral to executive presence. Your conviction in negotiation mirrors your belief in leadership.

- **Enhancing communication:** Negotiation hinges on effective communication. The ability to listen actively, understand underlying motivations, and articulate your stance succinctly is akin to a symphony of executive presence. Your negotiation prowess is a testament to your adept communication skills.

- **Strategic decision-making:** Navigating negotiations requires strategic thinking – assessing risks, evaluating alternatives, and making decisions that align with long-term goals. This strategic acumen, mirrored in negotiation, is a hallmark of influential leaders with executive presence.

## Strategies To Elevate Your Negotiation Prowess

Negotiation, like a dance, requires skillful steps. As you venture into negotiation scenarios, consider these strategies to elevate your negotiation prowess while advancing your journey toward executive presence:

1. **Setting clear objectives:** Approach negotiations with a clear understanding of your objectives. What are the outcomes you seek? Defining your goals aligns your negotiation strategy and ensures you stay focused and assertive.

2. **Active listening:** Listening isn't just hearing; it's understanding the nuances beneath the words. Pay attention to the other party's interests and concerns. This empathy-driven approach fosters collaboration and lays the groundwork for mutually beneficial solutions.

3. **Framing your stance:** Present your position not as an opposition but as a proposal. Frame your perspective in terms of benefits for both parties. This collaborative framing resonates with executive presence by highlighting your ability to navigate with strategic elegance.

4. **Flexibility:** While assertiveness is critical, flexibility is equally vital. Effective negotiation isn't about domination; it's about finding common ground. Being open to creative

solutions showcases your ability to pivot strategically – a mark of leadership.

5. **Building rapport:** Building a positive connection with the other party establishes a foundation of trust. Your genuine interest in their perspective demonstrates negotiation skills and interpersonal finesse crucial for executive presence.

6. **Conveying confidence:** Your body language, tone, and choice of words all convey confidence. Maintain eye contact, speak assertively, and use language that reflects your assurance. This confident demeanor mirrors the aura of executive presence.

7. **Leveraging silence:** Silence can be a powerful negotiation tool. Don't rush to fill every gap in the conversation. Allow silence to nudge the other party to offer more or rethink their stance. This measured approach highlights your strategic finesse.

8. **Seeking win-win solutions:** The hallmark of effective negotiation is a win-win solution. Strive for outcomes that benefit both parties. This collaborative approach resonates with executive presence by showcasing your capacity to lead for mutual gain.

9. **Embracing patience:** Negotiation is a process, not a sprint. Embrace patience as you navigate

discussions. Your composed and patient demeanor reflects executive presence, illustrating your capacity to navigate complex situations with equanimity.

As you harness these strategies, remember that negotiation is an art, not just a skill. It's the embodiment of your confidence, your assertiveness, and your strategic prowess. Each negotiation is a canvas where you paint the strokes of your leadership journey toward executive presence. With every deal you craft, every compromise you strike, and every collaboration you foster, you're sculpting an image of an influential leader who navigates challenges with finesse and shapes outcomes with unwavering determination.

## Up Next?

At this point, you're fully harnessing the profound power of assertiveness. Your confidence has evolved into an undeniable executive presence, propelling you to lead teams effectively, negotiate with finesse, and establish healthy boundaries. Armed with assertive communication skills, you're prepared to navigate pivotal work scenarios, foster collaboration, and steer your career toward influential leadership.

As you transition to the next chapter, you will delve deeper into the art of assertiveness by learning how to craft an indelible impression in job interviews, asserting your executive prowess. On top of that, you will explore strategies to shatter the glass ceiling during evaluation meetings, tackling gender disparities and forging an equitable corporate landscape. And finally, you will gain the essential tools for safeguarding yourself against workplace harassment while nurturing respect. Prepare to embrace your power and chart the path to unparalleled professional excellence.

# Chapter 12: Navigating Executive Terrain With Determination

Ready to learn the final vital part of your journey and transform your professional trajectory? Having journeyed through the realms of leadership and influence, you've honed the skill of assertiveness to craft a commanding executive presence. As you launch into this chapter, visualize yourself stepping onto the terrain of executive prowess, armed with knowledge and the strategies to navigate intricate career scenarios.

Now we will explore its strategic implementation across various career junctures. From making an indelible mark in job interviews to leveling up through evaluation meetings, I'll unravel the threads that tie assertiveness to your rise in the corporate hierarchy.

This chapter isn't just about skill; it's about empowerment. It's about equipping you with the assertive tools needed to break barriers, foster an equitable work environment, and protect yourself against the insidious forces of workplace harassment. As you delve into the intricate layers of assertiveness, remember that each concept and strategy contributes to a richer tapestry of executive presence. Brace yourself for an expedition into the world of assertive excellence, where every word, action, and decision is a step up on the ladder toward your professional prowess.

## Make Your Mark In Job Interviews By Emanating Executive Gravitas

In professional progression, job interviews are crucial milestones on your journey to executive leadership. These interactions are not merely assessments of your skills and experience but platforms for you to showcase your assertiveness, confidence, and potential as a future leader. This section delves into the art of mastering job interviews with assertive finesse, enabling you to emanate the gravitas of an executive-in-the-making.

## Unveiling The Art Of Assertive First Impressions

Your assertiveness takes center stage from the moment you step into the interview room. It's about walking in not as a candidate seeking approval but as a candidate ready to contribute meaningfully to the organization. The way you greet the interviewers, the firmness of your handshake, and the steadiness of your voice – all play a role in setting the tone for the conversation. Your assertive presence commands attention and establishes a foundation of confidence.

*Top Tip: Before the interview, practice your entrance. Stand tall, maintain a confident posture, and greet the interviewers with a warm smile. Visualize yourself exuding assertiveness and calmness.*

## Harnessing The Power Of Confident Verbal Communication

Words are your arsenal, and assertive verbs are the ammunition that propels your message. Every response you offer should resonate with intention and determination. Instead of saying, "I was part of a team that achieved success," assertively state, "I led a team to achieve remarkable success." By infusing your vocabulary with assertive verbs, you transform passive descriptions into dynamic accounts of your achievements and capabilities.

*Top Tip: Review common interview questions and practice framing your responses with assertive verbs. This exercise will help you convey confidence and authority in your answers.*

## The Eloquence Of Non-Verbal Assertion

Assertiveness extends beyond words – it finds expression in your body language. How you sit, stand, and move will communicate volumes about your confidence. Mastering the art of non-verbal communication is essential. Steady and direct eye contact reflects your self-assuredness. Employing power poses exudes authority. Controlled gestures emphasize your points. Together, these non-verbal cues amplify the impact of your assertive communication.

*Top Tip: Practice power poses and confident gestures in front of a mirror. Record yourself to assess your non-verbal cues and make necessary adjustments to enhance your assertive presence.*

## Responding To Challenging Queries With Grace

Challenging questions are opportunities to showcase your assertive problem-solving. Respond with grace and powerful honesty when confronted with inquiries about gaps in your experience or weaknesses. Rather than evading the question, use it as a chance to highlight your growth and adaptability. Your ability to navigate these challenges assertively underscores your readiness for leadership roles.

*Top Tip: Prepare responses for challenging questions in advance. Practice delivering these responses with assertive language and a composed demeanor to exhibit your ability to handle challenging situations.*

## Sealing The Deal With Assertive Closing Statements

As the interview draws to a close, your assertive closing statements leave a lasting impression. Express your enthusiasm for the role and articulate how your unique attributes align with the company's goals. A powerful closing statement isn't just a formality; it's a final opportunity to reinforce your executive presence and leave the interviewers with a compelling image of you as a future leader.

*Top Tip: Craft a strong closing statement that encapsulates your interest, value and assertive commitment to the position. Practice delivering it with conviction to leave a memorable final impression.*

In job interviews, assertiveness isn't just a trait; it's a transformative tool that elevates your candidacy. You shape a narrative of executive gravitas by embracing assertive first impressions, harnessing the might of confident verbal and non-verbal communication, gracefully navigating challenges, and delivering powerful closing statements.

# Navigating Evaluation Meetings: Assertive Strategies For Increased Gender Parity

In the dynamic realm of modern corporate culture, evaluation meetings have emerged as pivotal junctures where assertiveness can redefine your trajectory. Despite strides toward workplace gender equality, entrenched disparities in promotions and pay raises persist. A report by the World Economic Forum reveals that, on a global scale, women continue to face a substantial wage gap, earning only 63% of what their male counterparts earn. Moreover, women remain underrepresented in leadership positions, holding just 29% of senior management roles worldwide, according to a study by Grant Thornton. These sobering statistics illuminate the pressing need for assertive action.

This section of the chapter delves into the art of utilizing assertiveness as a potent instrument to dismantle the glass ceiling, address gender disparities, and proactively navigate the intricacies of evaluation meetings. This chapter will equip you with the assertive tools to catalyze extraordinary change within your professional sphere by unearthing research-based strategies and drawing inspiration from historical exemplars.

# • Assertive Self-Advocacy For Pioneering Gender Equality

Unfortunately, in modern workplaces, gender disparities still linger. Yet, assertive self-advocacy can become your imperative force for change. It's not just about expressing yourself; it's about wielding your voice as a compelling instrument to challenge and reshape prevailing gender norms. Research by Catalyst, a nonprofit dedicated to advancing women in the workplace, resounds clear: women who champion their accomplishments are significantly more likely to be considered for promotions and leadership roles. This finding, in itself, underscores the pivotal role of assertiveness in rallying gender equality.

The gender disparity in self-advocacy is starkly evident. A study published in the "Personality and Social Psychology Bulletin" reveals that women consistently rate their performances lower than equally performing men. This modesty often hinders them from assertively showcasing their talents and contributions. However, recognition of accomplishments is crucial. It not only impacts personal growth but also permeates systemic change.

## *Why Self-Advocacy Matters*

In the context of evaluation meetings, asserting your achievements is a strategic move that extends beyond personal ambition. McKinsey's "Women in the Workplace 2020" report highlights that women, particularly women of color, remain underrepresented at every level of corporate America. This extends to C-suite positions, where women hold only 21% of roles. By assertively communicating your accomplishments, you actively combat this underrepresentation. Your assertion challenges the status quo, compelling decision-makers to recognize and address the gender disparities that have persisted for decades.

Assertive self-advocacy is your assertion of worthiness, underscoring that you, too, are a driving force behind organizational success. In fact, a study by Zenger Folkman shows that women who effectively communicate their achievements are rated as more competent and are more likely to be recognized as high-potential employees.

## *Expanding Your Assertive Self-Advocacy Toolkit*

- **Craft A Compelling Narrative**

Beyond merely listing accomplishments, weave them into a compelling narrative that aligns with your organization's goals. Use facts, figures, and anecdotes to underscore your impact on projects, teams, and the company as a whole. Your narrative should radiate the ethos of a leader.

- **Embrace Confidence, Embody Presence**

Assertive self-advocacy is intertwined with confidence. Research published in "Organizational Behavior and Human Decision Processes" asserts that confidence is critical to perceived leadership potential. Practice confident body language, maintain eye contact, and assuredly speak during evaluation meetings.

- **Backed By Data**

Numbers carry weight. Quantify your achievements whenever possible. Did your strategies increase revenue? By what percentage? Did your leadership improve team efficiency? Specify the metrics. Such quantification reinforces the tangible value you bring.

- **Peer Support & Mentoring**

Don't navigate this journey in isolation. Engage with peer networks and mentors who can provide constructive feedback and guidance. A study by Harvard Business Review reveals that women with mentors are more likely to negotiate for promotions and raises.

- **Inclusive Language**

Your assertiveness should extend to inclusive language. Use "I" statements to own your accomplishments. This fosters an environment where your contributions are recognized and acknowledged without ambiguity.

- **Proactive Solution Presentation**

Beyond stating your achievements, propose future contributions. Outline how your skills can be harnessed for forthcoming projects. This underscores your commitment and proactive approach.

# • Using An Assertive Approach To Negotiate Your Career Trajectory

Assertive leadership thrives on negotiation—a skill that can reshape your professional trajectory. McKinsey & Company's research serves as a rousing call: women are statistically less likely than their male counterparts to negotiate initial salary offers, perpetuating wage disparities' persistence. These disparities reverberate through career trajectories, making assertive negotiation essential for dismantling such inequities.

## *Gender Disparities In Negotiation*

Let's delve into the sobering statistics: A study published in the "Journal of Organizational Behavior" reveals that women are 25% less likely than men to receive a raise when they ask for it. This disparity intensifies when it comes to promotions, with men being 85% more likely than women to initiate a negotiation for a higher position. The consequences of this are far-reaching. Over a 35-year career, the gender pay gap can lead to a cumulative loss of nearly $2 million for women. The gender pay gap also expands with seniority, with women at the executive level earning 71% of what their male counterparts earn.

## *Leveraging Assertive Negotiation*

Evaluation meetings morph into platforms for transformative change when approached with assertive negotiation. It's not merely about asking; it's about presenting an unwavering case grounded in compelling evidence. Fierce negotiation is a calculated dance—a strategic tango that demands meticulous preparation and confident execution. This is where your thorough research becomes pivotal. Whether striving for a promotion, a raise, or enhanced benefits, your assertive approach must be a symphony of substantiated facts.

- **Showcase Your Impact**

Illuminate the path you've carved within the organization. Highlight projects you've steered to success, quantifiable contributions, and initiatives that brought tangible benefits. These specifics speak louder than vague claims.

- **Market Your Proficiencies**

Your distinct proficiencies are your assets. A survey by Harvard Business Review unveiled that women often wait to be noticed, assuming their work will speak for itself. Break this cycle. Proactively tout your skills, emphasizing how they've enriched team dynamics and the bottom line.

- **Position With Market Data**

Arm yourself with market data. Use websites like *Glassdoor*. This site's "Know Your Worth" tool provides insights into what professionals in your field and position earn. This empirical data bolsters your negotiation with real-world context.

- **Anchor Your Request Aggressively**

Research from Columbia Business School demonstrates that ambitious anchor points in negotiation often lead to more favorable outcomes. Start your negotiation with a bold yet reasonable figure, allowing for a mutual compromise.

- **Leverage Peer Comparisons**

Highlight instances where your contributions surpass those of colleagues who have received promotions or raises. Comparative analysis can be a powerful testament to your value.

## Unleashing Organizational Change

Assertive negotiation is your catalyst for reshaping your career course and sparking systemic change. By breaking the chains of complacency, you create a domino effect that resounds across the organizational structure. Your assertiveness challenges biases, encourages transparency, and paves the way for an equitable workplace.

As you stand firmly in negotiation, you shatter the preconceived notions that have held back numerous talented women before you. Your assertive strides help reconstruct the narrative, heralding an era where negotiations are not seen as mere transactions but as pivotal steps toward gender parity. By championing your cause with unwavering assertiveness, you are not just negotiating for yourself; you are renegotiating the future landscape for all women who strive for equitable recognition and compensation. Your assertive negotiations today lay the foundation for a more inclusive and empowered tomorrow.

# Case Study — Parvati's Journey: Navigating Gender Dynamics In The Workplace

Parvati's professional journey unfolded within a predominantly male Engineering/Architecture consultancy company, where the gender distribution among professional staff was starkly imbalanced, with 90% male and a mere 10% female representation. This gender discrepancy was particularly evident among support staff roles, which were exclusively female.

In the earlier stages of her career at her company, Parvati experienced a supportive and professional work environment. Her managing director and previous team leader stood out as pillars of guidance and encouragement, especially during a challenging period when she battled clinical depression following the dissolution of her marriage. Parvati's resilience and dedication were unwavering as she consistently delivered projects ahead of schedule, displayed exceptional work ethic, and even played a pivotal role in establishing the company's Corporate Social Responsibility team.

However, the terrain shifted when her performance evaluation came into focus. Conducted by a new team leader and a director unacquainted with her role, this review marked a critical juncture. It was the second assessment in a span of three years, and initially, the process appeared promising. Parvati's accomplishments, including the successful completion of a £3 million project, positioned her as a high achiever.

Yet, the review took an unexpected turn. Under the category of "Communications or People Management," Parvati was advised to "flatten her personality" and "adopt a more passive demeanor." Curiously, these comments were not linked to any specific interactions with clients, colleagues, or contractors but rather pertained to her naturally exuberant and extroverted nature. Furthermore, she was criticized for not shouldering the responsibility for an error made by a former coworker before her tenure.

In her defense, Parvati professionally addressed these concerns, clarifying her stance on the oversight and expressing regret for not having authored the report in question. Her strengths as a "good communicator," diligent worker, and dedicated team player were also acknowledged.

This perplexing mix of feedback left Parvati in a state of bewilderment. Seeking guidance, she consulted her previous team leader who encouraged her to discuss the matter with the managing director. Consequently, her performance review was revisited, and the contentious comments were expunged.

The subsequent year introduced a new challenge. Managing eight distinct projects while reporting to two separate team leaders, Parvati grappled with conflicting demands. Her attempt to streamline communication and prioritize tasks by sending an email led to a clarifying discussion with both team leaders. This proactive move was noted in her review, albeit accompanied by a remark about occasionally feeling overwhelmed by concurrent projects.

During her subsequent performance review, Parvati confronted the issue of being labeled "overwhelmed" based on her email communication. A conversation with her team leader led to the removal of this characterization, which was replaced with commendation for her willingness to vocalize concerns and ensure timely execution.

Reflecting on her journey, Parvati couldn't shake the sense that her experiences were influenced by her gender. The comments about her personality, assertiveness, and handling of workload seemed to reflect biases that a male colleague might not encounter. While she considered the possibility of constructive criticism for growth, Parvati grappled with the notion that gender dynamics may have shaped the narrative of her evaluation meetings.

Ultimately, Parvati's story underscores the intricate interplay between gender perceptions and professional evaluations. Her journey prompts contemplation about the fine line between legitimate feedback and unconscious biases, reminding us of the ongoing endeavor to create a workplace where all voices are valued and empowered, free from the constraints of gender-based expectations.

## Catalyzing A Culture Of Equality

Assertive leaders aren't just forging paths of personal advancement but also trailblazers of progress for their peers. Your assertive drive can drive a workplace culture that not only welcomes diversity and gender parity but thrives on it. The rationale behind this transcends noble intentions—research consistently underlines that organizations with diverse leadership teams yield substantial advantages.

## The Business Case For Gender Parity

Let's unmask the empirical power of gender diversity. McKinsey's "Delivering Through Diversity" report paints a compelling portrait: companies in the top quartile for gender diversity on executive teams are 25% more likely to have above-average profitability. Another study by Peterson Institute for International Economics amplifies this, demonstrating a positive correlation between the presence of women in corporate leadership and increased firm performance.

## Breaking The Silence On Biases

The journey toward equal opportunity begins with candid conversations. The "Women in the Workplace" report by LeanIn.Org and McKinsey unveils that only 35% of women believe that promotions at their companies are fair. By boldly initiating discussions about biases and gender imbalances, you're addressing an issue that lingers unspoken in many workplaces.

## Assertive Conversations For Change

Your assertive aptitude finds new avenues here. Begin with raising awareness—share stories, data, and insights emphasizing diverse leadership's benefits. Then, drive the narrative towards solutions like these:

- **Advocate For Inclusive Policies**

Use your assertiveness to propel the implementation of policies that facilitate a level playing field. Champion flexible work arrangements, mentorship programs, and childcare support that ease the burden on women, enhancing their upward mobility.

- **Sponsorship & Mentorship**

Assertively spearhead initiatives that pair emerging female talent with mentors or sponsors. A Harvard Business Review study notes that sponsored women are 27% more likely than their unsponsored peers to ask for a raise.

- **Bias-Busting Workshops**

Pave the way for workshops that uncover unconscious biases. These sessions can be pivotal in sensitizing colleagues and leaders to their unintentional prejudices.

- **Inclusive Recruitment**

Imbue assertiveness into the recruitment process. Advocate for diverse interview panels, standardized evaluation criteria, and blind CV assessments to ensure a fair selection process.

- **Resource Allocation Transparency**

Assertively demand transparency in resource allocation. Ensure that high-impact projects, stretch assignments, and training opportunities are accessible to all, irrespective of gender.

## *The Ripple Effect Of Assertive Change*

By championing equality and balance, you're not merely addressing a concern; you're cultivating an environment where the assertive potential of all individuals can flourish. The powerful conversations you initiate lead to policies that dissolve roadblocks for women's advancement. Through your unwavering drive, you're amplifying a harmonious rhythm where each individual's assertive steps coordinate to create a collective crescendo of progress.

As you forge this culture of equality, you're building a legacy of empowerment. Those who come after you won't need to break down barriers; they'll find bridges thoughtfully constructed by assertive leaders like yourself. Your actions today set the stage for a future where diversity isn't just a buzzword but a lived reality and where women rise assertively, unimpeded by biases, into leadership roles that reshape industries and societies. Your assertive voice, united with those of your peers, harmonizes into a chorus of change that reverberates far beyond the walls of your workplace.

# Case Study — Madam C.J. Walker: The Fearless Sojourner Of Possibilities

In the annals of assertiveness, one name stands as a beacon of inspiration: Madam C.J. Walker, a true embodiment of audacity, determination, and triumph over gender barriers. Her life's journey, punctuated by adversity and defined by unwavering assertiveness, paints a vivid portrait of a woman who not only broke through ceilings but shattered them entirely, leaving an indelible mark on history.

### The Entrepreneurial Odyssey Of Madam C.J. Walker

At the turn of the 20th century, Madam C.J. Walker was born into a world far from gender equality. Yet, armed with an assertive spirit and an unrelenting belief in her potential, she transformed her circumstances. Rising from the ashes of poverty and discrimination, she established a beauty and haircare empire that defied societal norms and expectations.

### Breaking Barriers, One Strand At A Time

Madam C.J. Walker's assertive journey was an exercise in defying conventions. In an era when opportunities for women, especially African-American women, were severely limited, she strode assertively into the business world. She addressed a genuine concern by creating products catering to the unique needs of black women's hair. She challenged the status quo, asserting that everyone deserved to feel beautiful and confident.

### Pioneering Economic Empowerment

Walker's story isn't just about personal success; it's a testament to her assertive commitment to empowering others. As her business thrived, she employed thousands of women, offering them livelihoods and a pathway to fierce independence. By doing so, she irrevocably altered the economic landscape, proving that assertiveness isn't just about individual gain but also about creating opportunities that reverberate across entire communities.

### The Resonant Echoes Of Assertiveness

Madam C.J. Walker's impact wasn't confined to her time; it resonates today as a powerful reminder of what assertiveness can achieve. Her story underscores several assertive principles that continue to hold relevance:

- **Harnessing ambition:** Walker's assertiveness stemmed from her unapologetic ambition. Embrace your dreams with passion; they are the driving force behind your journey.

- **Empowering through enterprise:** Walker's business prowess was a conduit for empowerment. Your assertiveness can similarly manifest as a vehicle for uplifting yourself and those around you.

- **Unyielding self-belief:** Walker's assertiveness was grounded in her unwavering belief in her capabilities. Cultivate this belief within yourself, and watch how it propels you beyond barriers.

- **Amplifying voices:** Walker used her success to amplify the voices of others. Your assertiveness can create an echo that resonates through generations, inspiring others to assertively navigate their own paths.

### The Tapestry Of Empowered Assertiveness

Madam C.J. Walker's life is woven into the fabric of assertive history. Her story is a testament to the heights that assertiveness can reach, the barriers it can obliterate, and the legacy it can leave behind. As you embark on your assertive journey, envision Walker as your guide. This trailblazer beckons you to step boldly, assertively, and unapologetically into the realm of limitless possibilities.

# Protecting Yourself — Assertive Tools Against Workplace Harassment

In the intricate tapestry of professional life, the prevalence of workplace sexual harassment stands as a distressing reality. It's a challenge that transcends industries, hierarchies, and backgrounds and necessitates an assertive response. This section delves into the crucial realm of workplace harassment, revealing how assertiveness can serve as a powerful armor, fortifying individuals against such unwarranted behaviors.

### *The Ominous Shadow Of Workplace Harassment*

Despite advances in gender equality, workplace sexual harassment continues to cast an ominous shadow. A survey by the Equal Employment Opportunity Commission (EEOC) indicated that nearly 75% of harassment victims faced retaliation when they dared to speak up. Such statistics underscore the importance of assertive empowerment in facing such adversity.

## Assertiveness As An Antidote

Assertiveness isn't just a communication style; it's a formidable tool to dismantle the scaffoldings of harassment. It enables individuals to establish unwavering boundaries and, when necessary, to confront and address unwelcome behaviors assertively. By asserting one's rights and asserting the inviolability of personal space, assertiveness is a potent antidote against harassment's encroachments.

## The Assertive Response Blueprint

Assertively confronting workplace harassment requires a strategic blueprint. Here are some practical strategies that can serve as cornerstones for your assertive response:

10. **Define your boundaries:** Begin by assertively defining your personal boundaries. Communicate your limits clearly and unambiguously, leaving no room for misinterpretation.

11. **Confront with composure:** Should harassment rear its ugly head, confront the situation with composed assertiveness. Address the behavior directly and firmly, showing it's unwelcome and inappropriate.

12. **Document and preserve:** Assertiveness thrives on evidence. Keep a meticulous record of incidents, noting dates, times, locations, and

individuals involved. This documentation will be your assertive ammunition if further action becomes necessary.

13. **Seek allies:** Assertive strength is amplified in numbers. Reach out to colleagues, mentors, or friends who can stand with you assertively against harassment. Allies bolster your assertive stance and provide unwavering support.

14. **Escalate with assertiveness:** If the harassment persists despite your assertive efforts, escalate the matter. Engage relevant channels within your organization, such as HR or higher management, asserting your right to a harassment-free environment.

15. **Access external resources:** Assertive protection extends beyond organizational boundaries. Familiarize yourself with external resources, such as helplines, legal aid, or support groups, that can offer assertive assistance if internal avenues prove insufficient.

## Seeking Help & Support: A Bold Assertion Of Strength

In harassment-induced distress, seeking help isn't a sign of weakness; it's an assertion of strength. Recognizing the need for external support is fundamental to assertiveness in navigating such challenging circumstances.

- **Assertive dialogue with HR:** Human Resources (HR) departments are potent allies against workplace harassment. Approach them assertively, armed with your documented evidence, to initiate a formal complaint. Assert your right to a work environment free from harassment.

- **Legal recourse with assertiveness:** Assertive legal recourse might be necessary if internal channels falter. Consult legal experts specializing in harassment cases, asserting your rights to justice and protection.

- **Leverage advocacy organizations:** Numerous assertive advocacy organizations are dedicated to combating workplace harassment. They offer a network of support, legal guidance, and bold empowerment for those facing such challenges.

- **Constructive self-care:** Self-care is an assertive shield against the emotional toll of harassment. Engage in activities that nurture your mental and emotional well-being, asserting your right to heal and recover.

### *Embracing Assertiveness — A Strong Stand Against Harassment*

As you navigate the complex terrain of workplace harassment, assertiveness becomes your beacon of empowerment. It equips you with the tools to protect yourself assertively, set firm boundaries, and seek emphatic support when needed. By fostering an environment intolerant of harassment, you assertively contribute to transforming workplaces into realms of respect, equality, and assertive professionalism.

## Key Takeaways

The resounding theme of this chapter is clear: assertiveness is the lever that propels you toward an impactful career. It's not just about communication; it's about empowerment, breaking barriers, and shaping a narrative that aligns with your aspirations. By embracing assertiveness, you're not just navigating the twists and turns of your professional path; you're sculpting it, molding it to your vision.

As you move forward, keep this powerful arsenal close at hand. Apply these techniques, adapt them to your unique circumstances, and let them guide your every step. The power of assertiveness is now yours to wield, a mighty force that can chisel the stone of your career aspirations into a masterpiece of achievement. Embrace it, refine it, and watch as your professional journey unfolds with the fierce brilliance that only you can bring. Your legacy of assertiveness is enduring, lighting the way for those who follow in your footsteps. So, onward you go assertive trailblazer, for your journey has just begun.

# Conclusion

As our inspiring journey concludes, you stand at the threshold of transformation – a journey toward harnessing amplified confidence and embracing personal and professional assertiveness. The path to executive presence through these potent traits is now brilliantly illuminated by your determined strides.

Armed with newfound insights, you're ready to dismantle self-imposed limits and step out of the shadows of doubt. A life untouched by fear and where courage prevails is your rightful legacy. This book's interwoven stories of inspirational women testify to the power that blossoms when courage trumps apprehension. Embrace uncertainty; therein lies profound growth and the mindset to allow you to achieve your dreams. Let bold choices propel you, truth guide you, and steadfast convictions anchor your character.

Become the conductor of your own narrative. Skillfully nurture bonds at home, adroitly navigate connections with friends, and let your assertive voice rise even in the face of criticism or demanding situations.

In professional realms, master the blueprint of leadership excellence – gracefully navigate pivotal moments, say no when necessary, set boundaries, and wield the transformative language of assertive communication. Picture yourself radiating executive gravitas in job interviews and steering towards gender equality in evaluation meetings. Be a catalyst for parity, a sentinel against workplace harassment, protecting your dreams and aspirations.

Remember, the empowered self you've discovered is but the beginning of a lifelong odyssey. It's a commitment to embrace your inherent worth, authentic self and amplify your influence. Each day offers a chance to summon inner strength, wear authenticity unapologetically, and extend a hand to those seeking liberation from the situation you used to face.

A resounding call to action echoes – breathe life into your newfound knowledge. Cultivate environments where confidence thrives, and assertiveness is celebrated, whether at home, work, or in your community. Empower the women around you to rewrite their stories. Together, we solidify the bedrock of a future marked by parity and boundless potential.

And finally, with humility, I ask for your consideration. If this book has illuminated your journey, consider sharing your thoughts through a positive review. Your words can guide others on this transformative path. Through your advocacy, you hold the key to unlocking a cascade of transformation – an unstoppable tide of confident, assertive women surging forward, unwavering in the face of fear.

*If you enjoyed this book, please take a few moments to write a review of it. Thank you!*